THE WHITE SNAKE

The Lantern Festival (ensemble)

The White Snake

A Play

MARY ZIMMERMAN

Foreword by Mo Zhou

NORTHWESTERN UNIVERSITY PRESS
EVANSTON, ILLINOIS

Northwestern University Press
www.nupress.northwestern.edu

The primary source of this play, based on the ancient White Snake story, is a 1956 novel by Zhao Qingge called *The Legend of the White Snake,* translated by Paul White (New World Press Limited, 1998).

Photograph on page xviii copyright © Mary Zimmerman.

All other photographs copyright © Jenny Graham from the Oregon Shakespeare Festival production.

Printed in the United States of America

0 9 8 7 6 5 4 3 2

LIBRARY OF CONGRESS
CATALOGING-IN-PUBLICATION DATA

Zimmerman, Mary.
  The white snake : a play / Mary Zimmerman ; foreword by Mo Zhou.
    pages cm
  "The primary source of this play, based on the ancient White Snake story, is a 1956 novel by Zhao Qingge called The Legend of the White Snake, translated by Paul White (New World Press Limited, 1998)."
  Includes bibliographical references.
  ISBN 978-0-8101-2927-6 (pbk. : alk. paper)
  1. Bai she zhuan—Drama. 2. Folklore—China—Drama. 3. Love stories, Chinese. I. Zhao, Qingge, 1914– Bai she zhuan. Based on (work): II. Title.
  PS3576.I66w48 2013
  812.54—dc23
                          2013013226

To all the members of Team Snake; and particularly Bill Rauch,
whose idea it was.

CONTENTS

FOREWORD

Mo Zhou

This adaptation of *The White Snake* represents the culmination of a remarkable journey, one that began germinating thousands of years ago. As one of the four most popular legends of China, *The White Snake* is an epic love story that has been passed down through both oral and written traditions. Throughout its history it has been as shape-shifting as White Snake herself. One of the earliest recorded sources of the White Snake story is an anthology of classic folktales published in 981 C.E., which categorized it as a late period Tang Dynasty romance. The Tang Dynasty (618–907 C.E.) is known as one of the Golden Ages of China, and tales stemming from this period such as *The White Snake* firmly embedded themselves into the quintessential Chinese cultural fabric and provided crucial materials for future development. Hence, even after the chaos following the fall of the Tang Dynasty, the White Snake story continued to be dispersed and developed, remaining at the center of the popular folklore repertoire over the next seven hundred years.

At the end of the Ming Dynasty (1368–1644), the legend received its most prominent retelling. Feng Menglong's novella of the White Snake, entitled *Madame White Is Kept Forever Under Thunder Peak Tower*, was published in 1624. Differing from previous versions, Feng's tale was cast in the mode of formal realism, adding details of time, place, and character as well as local references. The story still focuses on a hapless young man, Xu Xian, who falls in love with a shape-shifting snake woman, Madame White. Although Madame White is ultimately a fantastical creature, she nonetheless decides to follow the societal expectations of a dutiful wife and only uses her supernatural powers to express her spousal d gratitude. In addition, Feng added incidents in which Madame White reveals herself as a white serpent, and for the first time introduced the character of Fa Hai, a Buddhist abbot. In Feng's account, Fa Hai magically traps both White Snake and her sister-maid, Green Snake, in an alms bowl and imprisons them under Thunder Peak Pagoda. Xu Xian becomes a monk and wills his own death several years later. In this telling Madame White remains a villain and Fa Hai the savior of Xu Xian.

The epic tale became immensely popular onstage during the Qing Dynasty (1644–1911). The first written script on record is a stage adaption from Feng's novella, *Thunder Peak Pagoda* by prominent playwright Huang Tubi. Huang was one of the first to exonerate the character of the White Snake. By introducing the concept of karma, he treats the marriage between Xu Xian and Madame White as predestined and beyond their control. As Madame White grew more sympathetic, Abbot Fa Hai's reputation cracked. In subsequent interpretations, the White Snake Lady has gradually evolved from a manipulative demon into an embodiment of love and compassion. Meanwhile her nemesis Fa Hai has transformed from a religious hero into a gruesome home wrecker, destroying the young couple's budding happiness and ignoring the true human affection that Madame White displays for her husband. At the same time, the depiction of Xu Xian is polarized: sometimes he is an innocent but sympathetic scholar, sometimes a fickle and lustful coward. Indeed, changes in its public reception have encouraged the story of the White Snake to shed many skins, each time revealing a new layer of humanity.

Karma, which brings the two lovers together, seems also to have sealed my personal connection with this production of *The White Snake*. Growing up in China, in fact in Hangzhou, the birthplace of the tale, I was soaked in this fantasy: walking past the Broken Bridge where Xu Xian and Madame White first met, paying respect to the spirit of Madame White at the Thunder Peak Pagoda, and—like all Chinese girls—imagining that I was one of the snake ladies and carrying out my own adaptation of the story with friends. In a word, the tale of the White Snake defines who I am today. Therefore, when I was invited to assist Mary Zimmerman on this production of *The White Snake* at the Oregon Shakespeare Festival, my heart skipped a beat. Words could not describe my joy. Known for her breathtaking adaptations of myths from various cultures, Mary simply is the most perfect person to introduce this story to a Western audience. Little did I know at the time that I was about to embark on a remarkable journey that would change my life artistically and personally.

This production of *The White Snake* was initially commissioned by Bill Rauch, the artistic director of the Oregon Shakespeare Festival. Like all Mary Zimmerman's productions, it began with no script at first rehearsal and developed over time. Yet this unique creative process is by no means sloppy. Instead it relies on thorough dramaturgical preparation and meticulous, disciplined execution. Our primary source for the text was the prose version of the tale by Zhao Qingge, written in the 1950s. Arguably the most underrated female writer in China, Zhao infuses the story with immense elegance. This book is one of the first translations of the story in modern Chinese. We also studied Wilt Idema's translation of *The Precious Scroll of Thunder Peak*. Written in 1908, *The Precious Scroll* includes all the recorded endings and subplots of the folktale. What is more, this particular book was written by a Buddhist monk, who writes in his preface, "Do not regard Madame White as a demon. She does not act like one. Should she not put to shame human beings who do not act like human beings but follow the ways of demons?" This is the first time the tale was retold by a religious figure, and his comment displays new insight into the deeper meaning of the story. We also studied Cecilia Zung's *The Secrets of the Chinese Drama* on the ritual of Peking opera. I have to admit that even though I am Chinese, I had not encountered these remarkable materials until I started working on this production, since they have been long ignored in China and were out of print. In other words, Mary went to great lengths to glean the materials that informed this telling, and she knows the legend to its core.

As director and adaptor, Mary writes for the particular actors she has cast. Only four central roles were assigned at the beginning—Lady White or Bai Suzhen, Green Snake (Greenie), Xu Xian, and Fa Hai. The rest of the ensemble members were expected to play multiple parts as the play developed. We were utterly fortunate to have the extraordinary ensemble from the acting company of the Oregon Shakespeare Festival. This diverse cast embraced the story with an open heart and displayed incredible faith in our journey. Mary would bring some new pages to each rehearsal, and we would explore them together. Often Mary began rehearsals with an idea for an image that would be central to the staging of the scene. The rehearsal room was always full of laughter and ideas. Because of its long oral tradition, the story line of *The White Snake* can be muddled as it contains trivial and sometimes contradictory details that were added by successive generations. Mary tightened the story by distilling the crucial dramatic conflicts; and, by using several ensemble members as narrators who posit differing explanations of the action, she manages to include multiple, even conflicting, versions of the story in one production, a genuinely masterful innovation in the storytelling of the White Snake. What struck me most is her fresh and profound understanding of the story. As a Chinese person, I often thought I knew the story too well. Nevertheless, at each rehearsal I found new layers and nuances sparking from the script. I will never forget the day when we reached the end of the story. Instead of pursuing a rather clichéd happy or melodramatic ending, or even any definitive resolution, Mary offers the most compassionate reflection of the story. When we finished reading the script for the first time, everyone was so touched that we could barely speak for sobbing. In a word, Mary pours her whole heart and soul into this unique vision. Under her guidance, the play, like a flower, grows petal by petal and reaches the most stunning blossom.

The reception of the production was phenomenal. Attesting to their love for the story, people would remain in their seats after each production, holding hands, smiling, and cherishing each other's presence in life. I was particularly moved when I learned that a legendary Chinese opera singer, who premiered the role of Madame White Snake in the 1950s, showed up at our revival performance at the Berkeley Repertory Theatre. After the performance she told the cast that it was the most compassionate and genuine production she had ever seen and thanked the team for respecting and carrying on the Chinese heritage. Indeed, since its publication thousands of years ago, *The White Snake* has enjoyed a growing popularity across the world. The story has appeared in countless translations and adaptations in different media, such as illustrated books, theater plays, Peking and other regional Chinese operas, films, TV series, and even a contemporary Western opera by composer Zhou Long, which was awarded the Pulitzer Prize for Music in 2011. Nonetheless no other production will hold as dear a place in my heart, not only because of the impeccable artistic integrity of the work but also the rare humanity that Mary Zimmerman unfolds from this ancient story. It reminds me of why I do theater in the first place and teaches me to savor each precious moment of my life. I hope that this profound play will also inspire you. After all, we all, in our own way, have a little white snake coiling in the most hidden part of our heart.

The White Snake had its world premiere at the Oregon Shakespeare Festival in Ashland, Oregon, on February 18, 2012.

The original cast was:

White Snake . . . . Amy Kim Waschke
Green Snake . . . . Tanya McBride
Xu Xian . . . . Christopher Livingston
Fa Hai . . . . Jack Willis
Sister and others. . . . . Lisa Tejero
Brother-in-Law and others . . . . Christofer Jean
Boatman and others. Vin Kridakorn
Crane Spirit and others . . . . Emily Sophia Knapp
Canopus and others . . . . Richard Howard
Acolyte and others . . . . Ako
Guan Yin and others. . . . . Gina Daniels

Musicians:
Tessa Brinkman: flute, alto flute, and piccolo
Ronnie Malley: pipa (Chinese lute), oud (Middle Eastern lute), and percussion—bass drum, tom tom, floor tom, frame drum, wood block, triangle, foot tambourine, shaker, Persian zarb, Chinese xiao shou and wuhan cymbals, and bao gongs
Michal Palzewick: cello

Daniel Ostling designed the set, Mara Blumenfeld the costumes, T. J. Gerckens the lighting, and Shawn Sagady the projections. André Pluess composed the music. Amy Warner and Karl Alphonso were the stage managers. Bill Rauch was the artistic director of the Oregon Shakespeare Festival. Mary Zimmerman was the director and Mo Zhou assistant director of the production.

A NOTE ON THE SET DESIGN

Following is a description of the original design for *The White Snake*. It is not meant to be prescriptive. Many other approaches could be taken. Very little is necessary to do the play.

When the audience enters, the stage is masked by a white silk curtain that will drop after the first line. The set appears to be made entirely of bamboo: a bamboo floor (painted) and two walls of bamboo framing the space, which appear to "lean out" away from the stage at a slight angle. The upstage "wall" is composed of a scrim in front of a screen. All the various locations of the story are embodied very minimally on this bare stage through, for instance, a shift in lights or the addition of a chair or stand of bamboo. There are, however, two additional design elements: rear projections on the upstage screen and a large Chinese medicine cabinet that rises from the floor to various heights. Three musicians are positioned at audience level off the front edge of the stage but fully visible. There is a set of stairs from the stage to the house.

Reflecting the characters' own ability to change shape, the two snakes are embodied in multiple ways: as a woman in fully human form, as a woman with a long snake tail trailing out from under her robe, as an undulating line of white parasols, as a single half-opened parasol, as a long snake puppet manipulated and spoken for by the actress playing the snake. All or none of these methods can be used to represent Lady White Snake and her dear companion, Greenie.

Various members of the company sometimes act as narrators of the play. Although in print the narration appears to alternate with the action or images, the two should always be simultaneous. Narration should not pause for action or vice versa unless specifically indicated.

The play was performed in one act; however, if you would like to try two short acts, the place to break for intermission would be at the end of the Dragon Boat Festival scene. We considered this, but never did the experiment.

Please see the appendix for additional details on the snake puppets, music, projections, and the cabinet.

THE WHITE SNAKE

CHARACTERS

White Snake (Bai Suzhen), a snake spirit
Guan Yin, a Bodhisattva
Green Snake (Greenie), a snake spirit
Xu Xian
Boatman
Sister, to Xu Xian
Brother-in-Law, to Xu Xian
Master Lin, a citizen
Master Liang, a citizen
Master Wu, a citizen
Fa Hai, Buddhist monk of Golden Monastery
Crane Spirit
Stag Spirit
Canopus, an immortal
Acolyte, to Fa Hai
Madame Lin
Second Acolyte, to Fa Hai

Additional roles include Narrators, The Moon, Merchant, Poor
Man, Doubt, Night Watchman, Visitors, Customers, Celebrants at
the Dragon Boat and Lantern Festivals, Water Spirits, Cloud Spirits,
and Dream Dragon.

OPENING

[*The* FIRST NARRATOR *sits in front of the silk show curtain. It is white, but a brush painting of bamboo leaves and the Chinese characters for "White Snake" are projected on it.*]

NARRATOR ONE:
Believe me

[*Music. The show curtain drops, revealing several members of the company seated in a row facing the audience. They slowly gather the fallen curtain in their hands.*]

NARRATOR ONE:
Once, long ago, in the middle of a great country

NARRATOR TWO:
Or, toward the southwest end

NARRATOR ONE:
There rose from the plains, and reaching to the clouds: a single, lonely mountain.

[On the word "rose" all the members of the company except the three narrators rise with the curtain so that it billows out, masking the entrance of another performer and WHITE SNAKE. *Then they drop it over those two so that it makes the shape of a mountain and foothills. The narration is continuous over this action.]*

NARRATOR THREE:
Not much grew there: some tree ferns, fir trees, cypresses, and pines.

NARRATOR TWO:
The winters were long up there,

NARRATOR THREE:
Adorned with icicles.

NARRATOR ONE:
And in this mountain, near the top,

[As the following lines are said, the silk is gradually drawn away.]

NARRATOR TWO:
There was a cave.

NARRATOR ONE:
And in this cave

NARRATOR THREE:
There lay coiled

NARRATOR ONE:
A white snake.

[WHITE SNAKE *is revealed. It is the performer, dressed in* WHITE SNAKE's *most elaborate human costume, manipulating the puppet version of the* WHITE SNAKE. *The puppet* WHITE SNAKE *is asleep, breathing gently.*]

She could have gone on there, sleeping her whole life through, as many of us do—

[*As the narration continues,* WHITE SNAKE *wakes up and begins to slither forward and "catches" a mouse offered by another performer.*]

NARRATOR TWO:
But, as many of us do, she sometimes felt there was another life for her.

NARRATOR ONE:
She glimpsed it sometimes, in the evening,

[WHITE SNAKE *stops and looks behind herself a moment, then moves on.*]

NARRATOR TWO:
Returning home with her mouse or her rat.

NARRATOR ONE:
Before settling down to sleep she glimpsed it,

[WHITE SNAKE *stops and looks around.*]

NARRATOR THREE:
Or felt it, just there, over her shoulder.

NARRATOR TWO:
Or rather, spine. Her little snake spine.

[WHITE SNAKE *keeps looking over her "shoulder" until she is curled on herself. She sighs and puts her tail over her head, depressed.*]

NARRATOR ONE:
And so, [WHITE SNAKE *gets an idea*] she decided she should study.

NARRATOR THREE:
Study the way of the Tao,

[*Two performers unroll a large scroll before* WHITE SNAKE. *Another holds a pair of spectacles attached to a long pole in front of* WHITE SNAKE'*s eyes.*]

NARRATOR TWO:
To find enlightenment.

[WHITE SNAKE *begins to study.*]

NARRATOR ONE:
She studied.

NARRATOR TWO:
And she studied,

NARRATOR THREE:
And she studied,

NARRATOR TWO:
And she studied,

NARRATOR ONE:
And she studied,

NARRATOR THREE:
And she studied.

NARRATOR ONE:
For one thousand seven hundred years.

[WHITE SNAKE *sighs and wipes her brow with her tail. Her glasses are removed.*]

NARRATOR TWO:
At last

NARRATOR ONE:
She became so enlightened she could command the weather,

[WHITE SNAKE *raises her head high. Thunder and lightning.*]

NARRATOR TWO:
Travel on the clouds,

[WHITE SNAKE *rises and zigzags through the air.*]

NARRATOR THREE:
Defeat demons in battle,

[*The puppet* WHITE SNAKE *circles the neck of* NARRATOR TWO *and stays there, as the performer* WHITE SNAKE *moves upstage.*]

NARRATOR TWO:
And most importantly, change her shape . . .

NARRATOR ONE:
Into that of a beautiful young maiden.

[*The performer* WHITE SNAKE *turns and reveals herself fully in her human form. Music ends.*]

MEETING GUAN YIN AND GREENIE

[*New music, the vamp for the song to come.*]

NARRATOR ONE:
Here is where the story of the White Snake begins.

NARRATOR TWO:
And immediately diverges—forks off, like a forked tongue.

NARRATOR ONE:
Some say—

[NARRATOR ONE *and* TWO *exit as* NARRATOR THREE *begins to sing.* WHITE SNAKE *is now represented by the company carrying and manipulating a line of open white parasols that increases in size toward the middle and decreases toward each end. This line is headed up by the* WHITE SNAKE *performer holding a parasol horizontally in a little less than half-opened position. This half-opened parasol has a ribbon on its top for a tongue, and two Chinese characters for eyes. It "breathes" gently, slightly opening and closing. Throughout the song, the* WHITE SNAKE *curls around the stage. Another performer, as* THE MOON, *carries an open white parasol held facing the audience. It travels slowly across the stage.*]

NARRATOR THREE:
One moonlit night
White Snake could not keep still.
Restless as the leaves that shimmer
In autumn breezes,
She coiled and uncoiled
Round and round the mountain,
When coming through the mist
Came the Compassionate,
The Bodhisattva Guan Yin.

[*Music ends.* THE MOON *travels slowly throughout the scene.*]

WHITE SNAKE:
My Lady Bodhisssattva!

GUAN YIN:
White Snake! What are you doing roaming the mountain this time of night?

WHITE SNAKE:
I confessss, I was trying to meditate, but I could not.

GUAN YIN:
Dear White Snake, your studies have brought you so far, you know how to fly on the clouds and change your shape; you are a skilled warrior—the immortals are all proud of you—and yet you have not transcended. Have you not wondered why? And why you are still so restless?

WHITE SNAKE:
I assumed, Lady Bodhisssattva, that your poor sservant has not yet had the patience nor the ssskill—

9

GUAN YIN:

That's not it. Let me tell you this. Before you were reborn on this mountain, many reincarnations ago, you were just a little snake in the mortal world, in the red dust.

WHITE SNAKE:

I wasss?

[NARRATOR THREE, *who has remained onstage, reveals a very small white snake hidden in her sleeve. She acts the part of the poor man here, as the performer who will play* XU XIAN *acts the part of the* MERCHANT *in this slight, suggestive reenactment from* WHITE SNAKE's *former life.*]

GUAN YIN:

One day you were caught by a poor man by the side of the road. He was just about to cut you in half to take your gall—

WHITE SNAKE:

Oh no!

GUAN YIN:

—when a timber merchant came by. When he saw what was about to happen his heart was moved, and—

WHITE SNAKE:

Why is that?

GUAN YIN:

What?

WHITE SNAKE:

Why was the merchant's heart moved by a sssnake on the side of the road? I thought that humans abhorred a snake.

GUAN YIN:

No one can say. There are few things so unsteady as those hearts of men.

WHITE SNAKE:

I sssee. Forgive my interruption. What happened then?

GUAN YIN:

He bought you from the poor man for one hundred copper coins and set you free, and that is why you have been able to practice self-cultivation to this day; the good deed of the timber merchant passed into you and made you something special.

[*The* MERCHANT *exits, fondly carrying the little white snake.*]

But now you must repay this favor—it is the only way to gain your final merit. Fortunately for you, that timber merchant has been re-born in the city of Hangzhou and his name is Xu Xian. Go there and serve this man as he once served you, and then you may at last join the ranks of the immortals.

[WHITE SNAKE *bows to* GUAN YIN *and departs.*]

NARRATOR ONE:

This is how one version goes. Others say it was not the Bodhisattva our White Snake met upon that moonlit night. That she never met the Bodhisattva, or heard about her past life with Xu Xian at all—

[GUAN YIN *departs, and the performer playing* GREEN SNAKE *enters with the* GREEN SNAKE *puppet.*]

But that she met someone else that night, an old acquaintance.

[*The* GREEN SNAKE *puppet attempts a flying trick, crashes into a wall, and falls in a heap to the ground.* WHITE SNAKE *has reentered, now only made of the* WHITE SNAKE *performer carrying the half-opened parasol head of* WHITE SNAKE, *always gently breathing.* THE MOON, *meanwhile, has returned to his starting position and will repeat his slow cross throughout the following scene.*]

WHITE SNAKE:
Green Snake!

NARRATOR ONE:
How to reconcile the two versions of the story? Let us agree: she only met the Bodhisattva in a dream. A dream she then forgot, but that we should remember.

WHITE SNAKE:
Green Snake! How hard at work you are!

GREEN SNAKE:
White Snake! How happy I am to see you! But how embarrassed: that you should see me, failing at the sword dance.

WHITE SNAKE:
You are an accomplished performer, but perhaps you could learn to be a little steadier . . .

GREEN SNAKE:
I'll say!

WHITE SNAKE:
It is only because of your impetuous nature. Later on, when your self-cultivation has reached a higher level, everything will be all right.

GREEN SNAKE:
Oh, I hope!

WHITE SNAKE [*suddenly a little awkward*]:
Green Snake, I hope you have forgiven me.

GREEN SNAKE:
Forgiven you for what, dear lady?

WHITE SNAKE:
In our contest of the magic arts—

GREEN SNAKE:
Oh forget it! It is only right that I should have lost—and badly, too! You've practiced so much longer than I, and so much harder. You've reached perfection!

WHITE SNAKE:
Dear friend, you flatter me.

GREEN SNAKE:
I've hundreds of years more to go before I reach your level. But I'm afraid I'll never get there. I have no patience. But what brings you out tonight? Usually you are serenely meditating at the full moon.

WHITE SNAKE:

I felt a little restless . . .

GREEN SNAKE:

Oh, I feel restless all the time. Living on this dreary mountain—there's no entertainment at all!

WHITE SNAKE:

Green Snake!

GREEN SNAKE:

I can't help it! You know that down below everything is so exciting.

WHITE SNAKE:

Yes, I've heard, and read about it too. But that is not for us.

GREEN SNAKE:

There's music and fine food and wine. There's all sorts of people and commerce, and beautiful sights to see. Don't you wonder sometimes what it is like? Sometimes I don't care about becoming an immortal at all. I just want to give it all up and get away from here—abandon myself to worldly pleasures.

WHITE SNAKE:

Oh, Green Snake, you shouldn't.

GREEN SNAKE:

Have you never felt the same?

WHITE SNAKE:

Well . . .

GREEN SNAKE:
Not even a little? A little bit? Or are you so very self-evolved?

WHITE SNAKE:
No, dear friend.

[WHITE SNAKE *sighs, and both she and* GREEN SNAKE *set aside the puppet versions of themselves.*]

I confess, in spite of my thousand years of cultivating the Way, I do feel restless sometimes. Even tonight—that's why I came out.

GREEN SNAKE:
You see? We can't help it.

WHITE SNAKE:
I wonder about those men in the ancient monasteries halfway down our mountain. Are they pestered by such distractions, do you think?

GREEN SNAKE:
The monks? Are you kidding? Those bald-heads go down the mountain all the time on some excuse or another, while we sit here piously self-cultivating.

WHITE SNAKE:
They do?

GREEN SNAKE:
All the time! They go for strolls by the lakes and see the cities . . .

WHITE SNAKE:
They do?

GREEN SNAKE:
Yes!

WHITE SNAKE:
And yet everyone admires them for their devotion.

GREEN SNAKE:
That's right.

[*Music, soft and longing.*]

Listen, dear friend; let's you and I go down the mountain.

WHITE SNAKE:
Oh, no . . .

GREEN SNAKE [*curling around* WHITE SNAKE]:
Just for a day, a single day? There would be no harm. It's spring-time—we should see the world—and then come right back up.

WHITE SNAKE:
No!

GREEN SNAKE [*continuing to entwine and curl with* WHITE SNAKE]:
We'll be back before anyone on this old mountain misses us. And don't you think that this is part of our cultivation? To know the world we are renouncing? We should know that!

WHITE SNAKE:
You think so?

GREEN SNAKE:
I know it! We'll go down in disguise; you as my lady, and I as your maid. What do you say? Just for one day!

WHITE SNAKE:
Well, perhaps there is no harm.

GREEN SNAKE:
No harm at all! It will be such fun!

WHITE SNAKE:
Well . . . all right then.

GREEN SNAKE:
Yes!

WHITE SNAKE:
But we must be disguised. And . . . what shall we call ourselves? We can't be called Snake this and that!

[*As they concentrate, they rise on their knees and undulate a little in unison.*]

GREEN SNAKE:
You're right. Let's call you . . . Bai Suzhen. "Lady White." Yes?

WHITE SNAKE:
Yes. And what about you?

GREEN SNAKE AND WHITE SNAKE [*thinking hard, hissing*]:
Sssssssssss—

GREEN SNAKE:

Greenie!

WHITE SNAKE:

Greenie?

GREEN SNAKE:

Plain and simple! And, only for one day.

WHITE SNAKE:

Greenie it is.

[*The music shifts; romantic, traveling music. Members of the company run forward carrying a large white or pale gray cloudy piece of silk raised high in the air.* NARRATOR FOUR *comes forward and hands* WHITE SNAKE *the full puppet version of herself.* WHITE *and* GREEN SNAKE *take their snake puppet versions of themselves and run upstage under the silk then turn as it descends and begin to cross it downstage, snaking their snake selves across its roiling surface.*]

NARRATOR FOUR:

Immediately they flew into the air and traveled through the clouds. When they began their journey they were snakes. But by the end, they were young maidens.

FLYING DOWN THE MOUNTAIN

WHITE SNAKE:

Dear friend, where shall we go? All of earth lies before us—how shall we choose?

GREEN SNAKE:

We might go anywhere, but . . . Once, I overheard a woodcutter who had ventured up our mountain. I remember that he sang, over and over: in the sky we have Heaven and on Earth we have Hangzhou.

[*They have traversed the silk. It is pulled forward up and over them again from the upstage edge as they run back upstage, temporarily masking them. When they reappear to cross a second time, the snake puppets are gone, and they are in their human form. They fly with their arms outstretched, leaning forward, stepping on one leg at a time and raising the other behind.*]

WHITE SNAKE [*repeating to herself*]:
"In the sky we have Heaven and on Earth we have Hangzhou."

GREEN SNAKE:

The West Lake is in Hangzhou, with isles and bridges, bamboo groves and gardens—oh, let's go there!

WHITE SNAKE:

Whereabouts does it lie?

GREEN SNAKE:

We'll know it when we see it. The lake is such a mirror up to Heaven, we'll see our own reflection, even at this distance: we'll look as though we're lying in a field of blue roses.

WHITE SNAKE:

There's no such thing!

GREEN SNAKE:

Then forget-me-nots?

WHITE SNAKE:
What a crazy little serpent you are!

GREEN SNAKE:
Oh no, madam, remember: I'm your crazy little *servant* now.

[*They are off the silk. It curls up over them again, led from the up-stage edge, as they run upstage. It is pulled away to reveal them landing.* WHITE SNAKE *alights gracefully while* GREEN SNAKE *sprawls on the earth. Music ends.*]

AT WEST LAKE

[*The sound of birds. A beautiful day. Various* VISITORS *to the park pass back and forth.*]

GREEN SNAKE:
Oh, madam, aren't you glad we came! Look at this splendor!

WHITE SNAKE [*feeling the ground, in wonder*]:
It's not "red dust" at all . . .

GREEN SNAKE:
Look at all the people, how they are hurrying by! They hardly seem to notice!

WHITE SNAKE:
They see it every day, I suppose.

[XU XIAN *passes by, carrying a red umbrella under his arm.* WHITE SNAKE *notices him and gazes after him.*]

GREEN SNAKE:

No excuse! What shall we see first? The Lingyin Temple? Or
Thunder Peak Pagoda?

WHITE SNAKE:

Thunder Peak Pagoda? I don't like the sound of that, somehow.
[*Looking where* XU XIAN *has exited*] Let's just wander—down to the
lake or by the gardens. Wherever our feet—

GREEN SNAKE:

Our new feet!

WHITE SNAKE:

Wherever our new feet take us!

[*Music. The park is filled with* VISITORS. WHITE *and* GREEN SNAKE
stroll arm in arm, very happy.]

VISITOR ONE:

So they meandered all day among that loveliness.

VISITOR TWO:

They heard the orioles sing.

VISITOR THREE:

The willow catkins fluttered in the air like swansdown or snowflakes.

VISITOR FOUR:

Pleasure boats plowed the field of the limpid lake, leaving shimmering furrows.

GREEN SNAKE:

Look, madam! The Broken Bridge!

WHITE SNAKE:
It isn't broken at all!

GREEN SNAKE:
No, they simply call it that.

VISITOR ONE:
On they went.

VISITOR TWO:
Morning turned to afternoon.

VISITOR FIVE:
The air was sweet.

VISITOR FOUR:
Fine moss grew in the shadows of pavilions.

[XU XIAN *crosses the path of* WHITE *and* GREEN SNAKE. *Everything stops. All the* VISITORS *stop in their tracks. The music becomes a sustained note.*]

VISITOR THREE:
And here our tale forks again, like the alternate forking paths of West Lake Garden.

WHITE SNAKE:
Greenie, have you noticed that young man with the umbrella?

GREEN SNAKE:
Indeed I have.

[*Everything resumes at a normal, lively pace.*]

So you are forming attachments already to the "dusty" earth in the form of that fine fellow?

WHITE SNAKE:
No, no. It's only that I feel I may have seen him before.

GREEN SNAKE:
And you would like to meet with him again?

WHITE SNAKE:
I think perhaps I might.

[*Everything completely stops again. The music is a sustained note.*]

VISITOR ONE:
And she pointed to the sky.

GREEN SNAKE:
Madam?

VISITOR THREE:
Was she merely pointing out that dark clouds had gathered, or did her pointing gather up the clouds?

GREEN SNAKE:
Madam?

VISITOR ONE:
In any case, it began to rain.

[*Music ends. One of the* VISITORS, *seated, lets rice fall from his hand into a metal bucket, a little at first then more and more. Concurrently, long, thin strips of pale blue silk unroll from the sky. First one, then two at a time, then a great many. It is the rain. All the* VISITORS *except the seated one flee the stage.*]

XU XIAN [*noticing the ladies huddling in the rain*]:
Young ladies! You mustn't stand about in the rain like this—the cold will cut you in half!

WHITE SNAKE [*as* XU XIAN *dashes over and holds his umbrella over them*]:
Oh sir, we thank you for your kind attention, but we are heading home.

XU XIAN:
May I be so bold as to ask: where do you live? Perhaps I could accompany you and offer you some poor shelter on the way?

WHITE SNAKE:
We ... uh ...

GREEN SNAKE:
Where do *you* live?

XU XIAN:
My humble home is by the Qian Tang Gate.

GREEN SNAKE:
That's where we live too.

WHITE SNAKE:
Near there, somewhat near: the Blue Billow Gate.

XU XIAN:
Well, then! I was about to hire a boat to hurry back across the lake—

WHITE SNAKE:
We won't trouble you further—

XU XIAN:
No trouble—

GREEN SNAKE:
May we share the boat with you?

XU XIAN:
I was about to ask the honor.

[XU XIAN *spots a* BOATMAN *with a long pole.*]

Boatman, please! Over here!

[XU XIAN *goes off to meet the boat.*]

WHITE SNAKE:
Greenie, this gentleman is so kind. Don't you think you should find out more about him—so that we may perhaps find some way to re-pay the favor?

GREEN SNAKE:
Don't you worry, madam.

XU XIAN:

Now, young ladies, if you will. Be careful here, climbing aboard the boat. Now, off we go.

[*Music. The ladies mount the boat, which is nothing at all, by pulling themselves along the* BOATMAN's *outstretched pole. The little party moves across the stage, swaying and stepping along in unison.* XU XIAN *holds his umbrella over the ladies. It is important that he not touch* WHITE SNAKE *during any of this journey. As they talk and travel this way and that, various members of the company pass slowly by, holding umbrellas.*]

GREEN SNAKE:

What is your name, sir?

XU XIAN:

My surname is Xu and my given name is Xian.

GREEN SNAKE:

So you are Master Xu Xian? Might one inquire as to Master Xu's occupation, and how he came to visit West Lake today?

XU XIAN:

I am an assistant in a pharmaceuticals store. I came today to pay respects to my parents' graves.

WHITE SNAKE:

Your parents are both deceased then, sir?

XU XIAN:

Yes, it is true. They passed away when I was young, and I was raised by my elder sister.

WHITE SNAKE [*to* GREEN SNAKE]:
Poor thing!

GREEN SNAKE:
Sir, how many members of your family are there? And may I inquire as to your age?

XU XIAN:
I'm twenty-three years of age. I live alone, with my sister and brother-in-law. I board with them.

GREEN SNAKE:
Not married, then?

XU XIAN:
Oh, no, no . . . I'm in no position . . .

WHITE SNAKE:
What a coincidence, sir, that you and I are both forlorn and wretched in this world.

XU XIAN:
Oh?

WHITE SNAKE:
I'm only nineteen years old, but alone as well. My father was an official who was slain by pirates, and my mother died of grief, of course. I have only my companion Greenie, here, to protect me from utter desolation.

BOATMAN:
Blue Billow Gate right ahead!

[*They arrive at the shore. The music ends.*]

XU XIAN:
Oh, here we are.

WHITE SNAKE:
And what a coincidence! The rain has stopped.

[*The lengths of silk drop to the floor. A moment of silence and stillness.*]

XU XIAN:
How beautiful the lake is after the rain, don't you think? Like a poem.

WHITE SNAKE:
Yes, it is.

[*A pause. Then as* XU XIAN *speaks, the company members quietly gather up all but one or two of the little puddles of blue silk, each gathering them into his or her parasol, and depart.*]

XU XIAN:
Well, I'm afraid I must be going. It has been a pleasure—

GREEN SNAKE:
Oh, mistress! I'm afraid it may rain again! And we'll be without protection. Don't you hear it? Hear it in the distance?

[GREEN SNAKE *gives the* VISITOR *a little kick, and he begins the sound of rain again.*]

WHITE SNAKE:
We must be going, also.

XU XIAN:
Take my umbrella.

WHITE SNAKE:
Won't you need it yourself?

XU XIAN:
Oh no, I'm nearly home. Please.

WHITE SNAKE:
But, how should we return it? Perhaps you could come to our house to fetch it.

XU XIAN:
Where do you live?

WHITE SNAKE [*looking around*]:
Not far from here—a red house on a corner to the west.

XU XIAN:
I'll come tomorrow.

WHITE SNAKE:
All right, then.

[XU XIAN *extends his arm with the umbrella.* WHITE SNAKE *reaches for it, and their hands touch. Everything stops. They are looking directly into each other's eyes. We hear a strange, ringing chord. Both of them begin to tremble. The trembling becomes so violent that* both of them and the umbrella are shaking. They are being drawn toward each other, as if pulled by a great force.]

BOATMAN:
Sir! We must get along.

[XU XIAN *and* WHITE SNAKE *break apart. The sound disappears.*]

XU XIAN:
Until tomorrow, then . . .

WHITE SNAKE:
Until tomorrow.

VISITOR/NARRATOR FIVE:
He departed into the mist. And our serpents slipped away also.

[*A brief moment of music.*]

[WHITE *and* GREEN SNAKE *gaze after* XU XIAN *a moment, then exit, in an S-shaped, snake-like pattern.*]

TWO HOMES (or, COMING HOME)

[XU XIAN *gathers up the remaining one or two lengths of blue silk and drapes them over himself as he enters his home. His* SISTER *and* BROTHER-IN-LAW *enter. His* SISTER *is carrying a tea tray with three cups and a little pot.*]

NARRATOR FIVE [*continuing*]:
Although Xu Xian was soaked to the bone, he had no regrets.

SISTER:
Good evening, little brother.

XU XIAN:
Sister. Honored brother-in-law.

[*They kneel for their evening tea.*]

BROTHER-IN-LAW:
Look at you dragging in all that water. Where have you been all day?

[XU XIAN *quickly takes off the lengths of blue silk.*]

XU XIAN:
Oh, I went to visit my parents' graves and sweep them.

BROTHER-IN-LAW [*noisily sipping his tea*]:
All day?

SISTER [*gently*]:
Husband—

BROTHER-IN-LAW:
All day it took you to sweep the graves?

XU XIAN:
Well, it was a beautiful day . . .

BROTHER-IN-LAW:
You call that squall that came up beautiful?

SISTER:
Husband—

BROTHER-IN-LAW:
And your sister left here with all the housework?

SISTER:
He works so hard at the pharmacy—

XU XIAN:
I apologize for my thoughtlessness—

SISTER:
No need—

BROTHER-IN-LAW:
Not enough sense to come in out of the rain.

[*Music.* SISTER *and* BROTHER-IN-LAW *leave.* XU XIAN *lies down to sleep, but he can't.*]

NARRATOR FIVE:
But nothing could diminish his secret joy. Xu Xian felt as if he had been asleep his whole life, and now suddenly he was awake to reality for the first time. Love feels like that when it comes. But remember that when it goes—when love ends—we have the exact same sensation: that we have suddenly awakened back to real life, and that love was the insubstantial dream. Which is it?

[*Music ends.* NARRATOR FIVE *exits.* XU XIAN *turns in his sleep.* WHITE *and* GREEN SNAKE *enter.* WHITE SNAKE *is carrying* XU XIAN'*s umbrella, open, resting dreamily on her shoulder.*]

GREEN SNAKE:

My lady! I don't understand! Why did you say we lived in a red house on a corner to the west? We have no such thing!

WHITE SNAKE:

Well, look here!

GREEN SNAKE:

This tumbled-down old place?

WHITE SNAKE:

It has a certain charm . . .

GREEN SNAKE:

Certainly—a hundred years ago! It might have been the house of a nobleman, but—

WHITE SNAKE [*uttering a charm and stamping her foot*]:
Mama mia hou!

[*A magical sound. The ruin is transformed into a beautiful, noble house.*]

GREEN SNAKE [*admiring*]:
Yes, this will do.

[*Pause.*]

My lady, I don't quite know what I should do. Should I remind you of the time and of our vow to be home by end of day?

WHITE SNAKE:
Why, it is the end of day. And we are home.

[*They look at each other and smile. Music.* WHITE SNAKE *plants the open umbrella upright in the stage, and it becomes the red house in the west. They exit.*]

MARRIAGE

[*Music. As* NARRATOR FOUR *speaks, a member of the company comes forward with a little sign hanging from her finger that says, in both English and Chinese "closed."* XU XIAN *rises, puts on an apron, and switches the sign to "open." A customer comes to the pharmacy with a shawl over her shoulders, her hands hidden.*]

NARRATOR FOUR:
The next morning, having hardly slept at all, Xu Xian arose and went to his job in the pharmacy. All day long he was not where he was. Wherever he looked, the image of her face, her eyes, her delicate hand appeared, like drops of rain rippling the surface of his day. Restless, restless Xu Xian. Finally, the long hours had crawled by.

[XU XIAN *flips the sign to "closed" and takes off his apron. As he crosses, the customer sheds her shawl, revealing long, long pointed nails. She is now* DOUBT. *The music shifts. Ominous.*]

But as he approached the red house in the west a new feeling came over him. A doubt was pulling at him.

[DOUBT *pulls at* XU XIAN, *plucking at his clothes, his hair, with her long nails, bothering him.*]

XU XIAN:

I might have known such a lovely young lady would live in such a beautiful house. But, how can I go in? Something isn't right. I shouldn't go in.

NARRATOR FOUR:

His heart was beating like a hundred buckets in an empty well.

[GREEN SNAKE *enters. Music ends.*]

GREEN SNAKE:

Master Xu! What are you doing coming here and then running away again!

XU XIAN:

I, uh . . .

GREEN SNAKE [*approaching and shoving* DOUBT *away*]:

My lady was afraid you wouldn't be able to find the house and sent me out to watch for you. Now come along! She's waiting.

[*Music.* NARRATOR FIVE *enters as* GREEN SNAKE *pulls* XU XIAN *off. He is wearing spectacles and carrying a book,* Secrets of the Chinese Drama.]

NARRATOR FIVE [*reading*]:

Secrets of the Chinese Drama, Chapter Eight: "How a Host Seats Her Guests, or, *Wa Men.*" Part One. When the Host and the Guest Enter Through Different Doors.

[*As* NARRATOR FIVE *reads, two chairs are brought forward.* XU XIAN *and* WHITE SNAKE *enter from opposite sides of the stage and complete each of the actions described.*]

The Guest comes on the stage through S, while the Host enters through H. They are to greet each other at C. They then move in complementary circles, circumnavigating point C until they come to point D where they again exchange greetings, the Host asking the Guest to take A—the seat of honor—and the Guest modestly refusing. Finally, they proceed to take their seats.

[NARRATOR FIVE *exits. Music ends. Both* WHITE SNAKE *and* XU XIAN *feel shy.* XU XIAN *is overwhelmed by the grandeur of the place, and he feels he doesn't belong.*]

WHITE SNAKE:
So Master Xu, you are a man of your word, I see.

XU XIAN:
Honorable Lady, I . . . I thank you, and—

WHITE SNAKE:
Please don't stand on ceremony, sir. I hope you will make yourself at home here and put yourself perfectly at ease.

XU XIAN:
You certainly— [*he is about to say "are beautiful" but catches himself*] it certainly is such a lovely house.

[*Pause. An ecstatic shyness on both their parts. It is unbearable.*]

WHITE SNAKE [*calling*]:
Greenie! Please bring some wine and snacks for Master Xu that we may show our gratitude to him.

XU XIAN:

Please. I beg of you, don't go to any trouble on my account. I do not deserve nor can I return such hospitality. I really must be going—

WHITE SNAKE:

Oh sir, you must reconsider. Although our acquaintance is not of long standing it was surely fate that we share your boat yesterday in the rain. I confess, it would have been devastating to my feelings if you had refused.

[GREEN SNAKE *enters with a small table with a small jug of wine and two cups that she places between the two chairs.*]

XU XIAN:

Your kindness overwhelms me.

GREEN SNAKE [*offering* XU XIAN *a cup of wine*]:
Don't mention it, sir.

[*Music: song.* NARRATOR TWO *passes by. As he sings,* XU XIAN *and* WHITE SNAKE *drink more and more wine, served by* GREEN SNAKE. *They relax, laugh, steal glances at each other. The light shifts and slides across the floor. By the end of the song, it is evening.*]

NARRATOR TWO [*singing*]:
The evening light slides along the floor.
Across the meadow each blade of grass
Is robed in saffron and jade.
The sun drops gently behind the hill
Like the eyes of our Lady Bai
Drop as she glances at Xu Xian.
Time disappears among friends.
Time disappears among friends.

[NARRATOR TWO *exits.*]

WHITE SNAKE:
Greenie, may I speak to you?

[WHITE *and* GREEN SNAKE *draw away from* XU XIAN *while he continues to enjoy his wine.*]

GREEN SNAKE [*with mock seriousness*]:
So, my lady, do you wish me to send him away?

WHITE SNAKE:
You know that isn't it!

GREEN SNAKE [*carrying on*]:
Oh, you wish me to detain him? How shocking!

WHITE SNAKE:
Stop pretending!

[GREEN SNAKE *laughs.*]

You know what is in my heart—surely you can see it! Oh, Greenie, act as my go-between, will you?

GREEN SNAKE [*sober again*]:
Your go-between for what?

WHITE SNAKE:
Stop it! You know very well what I mean.

[GREEN SNAKE *laughs and laughs.*]

GREEN SNAKE:
Of course I will!

WHITE SNAKE:
Now, Greenie, one more thing. If we are to stay in the world of mortals, we will need money. I need you to go tonight and "borrow" some.

GREEN SNAKE:
How? From whom?

WHITE SNAKE:
I've heard that the money in the magistrates' office is all obtained by extortion and corruption. Why should we not get a little ourselves?

GREEN SNAKE:
Oh I see! So you want me to "borrow" this government money?

WHITE SNAKE:
You understand me perfectly.

GREEN SNAKE:
Oh, wonderful! You'll see—I'll demonstrate my skills in the magic arts. But, first things first: leave me alone with the young man.

[WHITE SNAKE *departs, taking the small table.* XU XIAN *watches her go.*]

So, Master Xu, what do you think of our home, sir?

XU XIAN [*slightly drunk*]:
It's so very dazzling. Like a dream.

GREEN SNAKE:
Since you like it so much, why don't you stay?

XU XIAN:
—?—

GREEN SNAKE:
Let's not beat about the bush, Mr. Xu. Isn't it time you were married
with a home of your own?

XU XIAN [*astonished*]:
Why no! It's out of the—I can't afford—to, uh . . .

GREEN SNAKE:
I think I might know a certain young lady who would be honored to
wed herself to such a one as you.

XU XIAN:
That is very kind of you, but just whom do you have in mind?

GREEN SNAKE:
You can't guess?

XU XIAN:
Why, no.

GREEN SNAKE:
No one comes to mind?

XU XIAN:
Dear maid, I'm at a loss—?

GREEN SNAKE:
My mistress of course!

XU XIAN [*astonished*]:
Your mistress? Lady Bai?

GREEN SNAKE:
Yes, of course.

XU XIAN:
Dear maid! Please do not make a joke of your humble guest.

GREEN SNAKE:
Who says I'm joking?

XU XIAN:
Please, dear maid, I have no rank at all.

GREEN SNAKE:
Listen, the truth is, my mistress was once, long ago, betrothed to a young nobleman. But because he was so wealthy he was idle, and his idleness led to certain . . . bad habits—I needn't elaborate—that led to illness that carried him off. After that, in her devastation, she took a solemn vow that if she were ever to consider marriage again, it would only be to someone of low birth. Someone interested in trade or . . . agriculture. Now, at last, it has come about that she has taken a fancy to you, sir. In fact, it was love at first sight. What do you say?

XU XIAN:
I'm deeply grateful for your kindness, Greenie, and for acting as the go-between. But, you must understand: not only am I not noble, I

am a poor man—living under another's roof, in fact. Even if it is—were—even if it were my heart's desire, how could I harbor such a wild hope as to marry your—?

GREEN SNAKE:
Oh, sir, my mistress values honesty, integrity—and generosity such as you showed yesterday. She has an inheritance. Once the two of you are married you can move into this house and have no worries at all.

XU XIAN:
This is all so sudden. I don't know what to say.

GREEN SNAKE:
There is nothing to say but yes. Say yes.

XU XIAN:
But . . .

GREEN SNAKE:
Master Xu, just say yes.

XU XIAN:
In that case, I express my deepest thanks.

[XU XIAN *bows deeply. At that moment comes the sound of the* NIGHT WATCHMAN's *bell.* DOUBT *springs forward and begins to torment* XU XIAN *again. Throughout the following scene the* NIGHT WATCHMAN *crosses the stage upstage slowly ringing his bell.*]

Good heavens! It is midnight already—I must be going.

GREEN SNAKE:
There won't be a boat this time of night.

XU XIAN:
I'll look around. Or, I can walk the long way around . . .

GREEN SNAKE:
You haven't a lantern.

XU XIAN:
The moon is full.

GREEN SNAKE:
No, but it's cloudy—it's clouding up.

XU XIAN:
I'll find my way. Please give my warmest—

GREEN SNAKE:
The road is treacherous at night—with bandits and . . . construction.

[WHITE SNAKE *peers in, listening.*]

XU XIAN:
My dear maid, I must be going. Please give my apologies to—

GREEN SNAKE:
Why not marry my mistress right now? It would save so much trouble.

XU XIAN:
Dear maid, this is a matter of such importance. There are so many things to do. I must go and speak to my sister and brother-in-law.

Then bring the wedding present, choose an auspicious day and time, and all the rest of it.

[GREEN SNAKE *pulls the red umbrella from the stage and offers it to* XU XIAN. *The* NIGHT WATCHMAN *and his bell are gone.*]

GREEN SNAKE:
You've already given a wedding present: the umbrella! Who cares about your sister and your brother-in-law! They are not your parents! You don't need their permission! What are you—a baby? You can't make your own decisions?

[DOUBT *backs off.*]

WHITE SNAKE [*entering, innocently*]:
Forgive my absence, Master Xu—why, what is going on?

GREEN SNAKE:
Master Xu has something to ask you, my lady.

WHITE SNAKE:
Oh?

GREEN SNAKE:
Don't you?

XU XIAN [*suddenly decisive, while still a little tipsy*]:
Yes. I do. Miss, I wish to spend a lifetime of happiness together with you. I pray that you will not refuse me.

WHITE SNAKE:
I think it is an excellent idea.

XU XIAN [*astonished, but continuing*]:
And further, I wish that we do not delay, but conduct the ceremony now. This very night.

WHITE SNAKE:
You have spoken my own heart's desire.

[*Music: song.* NARRATOR THREE *sings. During the song a large wedding ribbon falls from the sky. Two company members come forward to take the chairs and act as the ancestors who bow and are bowed to by the lovers at the appropriate moment. The ancestors depart as* GREEN SNAKE *comes forward with the ribbon and gives each of the lovers one end of it. She exits as* WHITE SNAKE *draws* XU XIAN *toward her with the wedding sash. They begin to walk off together.*]

NARRATOR THREE:
My heart is blooming
Like a thousand flowers.
To Heaven and Earth we bow.
And now to our ancestors,
Bless us if you will.
This night and forever I to you am bound.

[*The two lovers become entwined with the ribbon and with each other.* NARRATOR THREE *exits, and* NARRATOR FIVE *enters. The music of the song continues.*]

NARRATOR FIVE:
I've heard it said that we fall most deeply in love when the other person seems to open a door to an entire world we have not known. For Xu Xian, though he didn't know it, Bai Suzhen held the key to

all the mystery and the shadows of the unseen world. And for Bai Suzhen, he carried all the treasure of this one. All the sunlight, and the grass in the breeze were in him. And in both was an identical loneliness. That lifted, this night, for the first time in centuries.

[*The music shifts, becomes more driven and sneaky. As the lovers are entwined,* GREEN SNAKE *enters in the form of a long line of green parasols that weave about the stage and circle the lovers. Then* GREEN SNAKE *in puppet form is revealed inside the coils. The parasol version departs.* GREEN SNAKE *slithers to a wall, strikes it with her snout, and a small door opens. She half enters the hole, waving her tail. Three bags of gold ingots fly out one by one from the hole.* GREEN SNAKE *puppet enters the wall fully.* GREEN SNAKE *performer is left onstage, and she shuts the little door. Music ends.* WHITE SNAKE *rises and sees* GREEN SNAKE. *We are back in the red house.*]

WHITE SNAKE:
Three thousand ounces! You've surpassed yourself!

GREEN SNAKE:
If I hadn't used my magic arts it would have taken two people with axes to chop a hole in the wall. As it is, I left no mark at all!

[GREEN SNAKE *laughs and drops all the ingots on the floor.*]

XU XIAN [*waking*]:
My goodness—the sun is so high! What time is it? I'll be late for the pharmacy!

[XU XIAN *stands but can't untangle himself from the red wedding sash. He is in a panic.*]

WHITE SNAKE:
Husband—

XU XIAN:
Forgive me, I— [*Seeing the ingots*] What's this?

WHITE SNAKE:
Dear husband, this is my inheritance, and now it is yours as well. Sit down a moment—

XU XIAN:
Forgive me, I must go. I will lose my employment!

[XU XIAN *hurries to leave but stops when* WHITE SNAKE *speaks. He straddles the threshold of her home, one foot inside and one foot back in the world.*]

WHITE SNAKE:
Husband, just one moment. Listen to me. There is no future in being an assistant. The only way to get ahead in this world is to be in business for oneself. Take this money and open your own pharmacy! I know something of the healing arts myself—we will do very well.

XU XIAN:
But I've never run a business before.

WHITE SNAKE:
Nor have you ever married before, or even been to this house which is now yours, before last night.

XU XIAN:
It's true.

WHITE SNAKE:
It's a new life, dear husband. Don't you see? You are no longer a lowly pharmacist's assistant. Overnight, you've shed your skin.

XU XIAN:
I have?

WHITE SNAKE:
Like a snake, my love, like a snake.

OPENING THE PHARMACY AND THE COMING OF FA HAI

[*Music. During the following narration,* WHITE *and* GREEN SNAKE *gather the ingots and go off. A cabinet rises from the stage floor to counter height;* XU XIAN *checks its drawers and polishes it with great energy and happiness.*]

NARRATOR TWO:
The plan was a very good one. Xu Xian found a fine location for the pharmacy and set about the task of construction, using the capital of the stolen ingots. Meanwhile Bai Suzhen ordered all the ingredients she would need to heal any sickness; many of these ingredients were strange and unheard of in medical practice—

[XU XIAN *opens a jar and lifts out a very strange ingredient.*]

But she knew what she was doing. Greenie was in charge of advertising, for which she was well suited—

GREEN SNAKE [*offstage, loudly*]:
Bao He Pharmacy!

NARRATOR TWO:
—because she was not shy. The two ladies determined they should live inconspicuously among the mortals of this world, and earn their money honestly in the future.

[GREEN *and* WHITE SNAKE *reenter dressed in more humble clothes.* GREEN SNAKE *ties an apron around* WHITE SNAKE*'s waist.*]

The trio moved in above the shop as soon as it was finished.

[*A company member enters holding a little bell and with the open/ closed sign hanging from her finger.* XU XIAN *turns it to "open."*]

A bright and glorious spring was unfolding a picture of radiant prosperity as Bai Suzhen and Xu Xian opened the Bao He Pharmacy.

[*The music picks up as customers begin to arrive at the shop with various ailments, first one by one but then in increasing numbers.* WHITE SNAKE *pulls remedies from the cabinet and cures the customers quickly as* XU XIAN *gathers money.* GREEN SNAKE *brings more customers through the "door"—which is the company member with the open/closed sign and the little bell, which she rings with each entrance and exit. The cabinet rises to its full height, and* XU XIAN *dons a beautiful robe, both signs of the growing prosperity of the pharmacy. Finally, all the customers are gone, and the music slows. It is the end of a day and the trio tidy up.* NARRATOR THREE *enters and begins her song, during which* WHITE SNAKE *disappears briefly behind the cabinet and reemerges, clearly pregnant.* GREEN SNAKE *exits.*]

NARRATOR THREE:
Your steps are slowing, sweet Lady Bai,
And why are you ill in the morning?
There is one sickness that we all long for
And it's cured by a baby crying.

[*Music ends.*]

XU XIAN [*as* WHITE SNAKE *bends to pick up some debris*]:
My love; be careful! You can't continue to work these long hours in your condition. We can get along very well just selling the medicines—you needn't treat people yourself.

WHITE SNAKE:
Oh, I have several months yet before we need worry. It's true, we started the pharmacy to make money, but what is important is to treat the patients.

XU XIAN:
Nonetheless, come up now and rest.

[*They exit.* NARRATOR TWO *enters carrying a golden parasol. Music begins and the cabinet sinks back into the ground.*]

NARRATOR TWO:
Day after day they lived in tender sunlight. Their happiness increased as word of Lady Bai's abilities spread far and wide. Perhaps too far; as far as the Golden Monastery.

[*The music darkens considerably.* NARRATOR TWO *plants the golden parasol upright in the stage to signify the Golden Monastery. Three citizens enter, two together and a third, limping and breathing heavily, following. They are visiting the temple, with sticks of incense in hand. Throughout their conversation they will offer incense and pray a little; and throughout the entire scene we hear the constant, somewhat distant sound of a low, reverberant bell or gong being struck every five seconds or so.*]

Here is how it happened. One day, three citizens met while offering incense.

MASTER LIN:
Master Liang! How nice to see you. Returned from your travels?

MASTER LIANG [*politely, but in physical distress*]:
Master Lin, Master Wu . . .

NARRATOR TWO:
Now this Golden Monastery was the home of one Fa Hai.

[FA HAI *enters.*]

This holy man was far advanced in enlightenment: he could see the past and future and was skilled in magic arts. But although he could recite scripture, he had a villainous heart.

[FA HAI *seems to trap a little butterfly tenderly in his hand, then he tosses it on the floor and crushes it with his staff. Then he sits apart from the citizens, scowling.*]

MASTER LIN:
Why, you don't seem well, Master Liang, is something ailing you?

MASTER LIANG [*wheezing*]:
I've been having trouble with my breathing of late.

MASTER WU:
Have you been to the new Bao He Emporium?

MASTER LIANG:
Why, no.

MASTER WU:
You must go right away. They can cure anything!

MASTER LIANG:
Oh?

MASTER LIN:
My niece turned yellow and had a bloated belly—Lady Bai fixed the matter in three days!

FA HAI [*overhearing, to self*]:
Lady Bai?!

MASTER WU:
Master Lee couldn't move his right eye and began to grow a horn.

MASTER LIN:
Gone!

MASTER WU:
Gone in an hour!

MASTER LIN:
There was the outbreak of pestilence—

52

MASTER WU:
We all had it! You're lucky you weren't here.

MASTER LIN:
But Lady Bai treated everyone with a special elixir.

FA HAI:
Lady Bai?!

MASTER LIN:
No one knows what's in it.

MASTER WU:
But it cured everyone—and she didn't charge!

MASTER LIANG:
Didn't charge!

MASTER WU:
She says it's easy for her.

MASTER LIN:
Her powers seem almost magical.

FA HAI [*to self*]:
I'll say!

MASTER LIN:
You must go immediately! Lady Bai at the Bao He Emporium. She runs it with her husband, Xu Xian.

MASTER LIANG:
I'll go right away.

FA HAI [*lightly kicking* MASTER LIN]:
You there!

MASTER LIN [*terrified*]:
Honorable Abbot Fa Hai.

FA HAI:
Have you paid your incense money?!

MASTER LIN [*timidly*]:
Why, yes. In fact, Honorable Abbot, if I am not mistaken, you owe me change from last week.

[MASTER LIN *puts out his hand.*]

FA HAI:
I don't recall that.

MASTER LIN:
No, indeed. Nor do I, Abbot. We'll be on our way.

[MASTERS LIN, LIANG, *and* WU *exit quickly. Ominous music.*]

FA HAI:
I knew it! I sensed a miasma of demonic spirits hovering over the town. By my calculations this Lady Bai must be the White Snake spirit missing from Mount Emei. How dare she! How dare she slither down the mountain and stick her snout into the affairs of humans! Pretending to bring benefits to people by dabbling in medicine: it's nothing but her trickery. And taking a mortal husband! We'll see about that! *This is Buddha's country!*

[*Music ends.* FA HAI *exits.*]

NARRATOR TWO:
And off he went. And off our story goes.

[NARRATOR TWO *exits. The cabinet rises.* GREEN SNAKE *enters, sweeping. She sees a bug in the dust and eats it.* XU XIAN *enters carrying a basket of peaches.*]

XU XIAN:
Greenie, where is Lady Bai?

GREEN SNAKE:
Upstairs resting.

[XU XIAN *knocks on the cabinet door. It opens to reveal a "bedroom" with* WHITE SNAKE *reclining.* GREEN SNAKE *continues sweeping.*]

XU XIAN:
My dear, am I disturbing you? I brought you something.

WHITE SNAKE:
Oh, too sweet!

XU XIAN:
Peaches.

WHITE SNAKE:
Yes, peaches—you do too much for me!

XU XIAN:
What are you saying? Compared to what you've done for me . . .

WHITE SNAKE [*reaching into the basket*]:
What's this?

XU XIAN:
A pomegranate blossom, for your hair. Look [*putting the flower in her hair*]—even more gorgeous and alluring.

WHITE SNAKE [*uneasy*]:
Ah, so the pomegranates have bloomed already?

XU XIAN:
Mm hm. The Dragon Boat Festival is just around the corner.

WHITE SNAKE [*trying to seem casual*]:
It is?

XU XIAN:
Yes—our first together. We'll drink our realgar wine and chase those demons away—how about that?

[FA HAI *has entered the shop.* GREEN SNAKE *addresses him.*]

GREEN SNAKE:
May I help you?

WHITE SNAKE:
I don't care for that festival.

FA HAI:
What? No.

XU XIAN:
You seem out of sorts. You need your rest.

[XU XIAN *closes the cabinet doors and exits to behind the cabinet.*]

GREEN SNAKE:
Are you here to buy medicine or beg for alms?

[FA HAI *doesn't answer, keeps poking around.*]

Excuse me?

FA HAI:
Is there someone of higher rank I may speak to?

GREEN SNAKE:
Higher rank?

FA HAI:
Yes, why don't you fetch a proper person?

GREEN SNAKE:
Yes, why don't you fetch your fat old bald head out of here?

FA HAI:
I believe Master Xu is the proprietor?

GREEN SNAKE:
Don't trip on your little girly robes on the way out.

XU XIAN [*entering from around the cabinet*]:
Greenie! Why don't you see if Lady Bai needs anything?

[GREEN SNAKE *goes off.*]

Now, reverend sir, may I ask what I can do for you?

FA HAI:

Are you Xu Xian—Xu the proprietor?

XU XIAN:

I am.

FA HAI:

Amithabha Buddha! I'm the abbot of Golden Mountain Temple. I have something important to tell you. Is there somewhere convenient for us to talk, or shall we go outside for a stroll?

XU XIAN:

Forgive me for not recognizing the esteemed Fa Hai; come have a seat in the guest room. Greenie!

[*Music.* NARRATOR FIVE *enters wearing spectacles and carrying his book,* Secrets of the Chinese Drama. *As he reads, two chairs are brought forward and* FA HAI *and* XU XIAN *perform all of the actions described.*]

NARRATOR FIVE:

Secrets of the Chinese Drama. Chapter Eight, Part Two. "How a Host Seats His Guest When Entering Through the Same Door." The Host leads the Guest to the front center of the stage, reverses, crosses the threshold, and turns left towards S, while the Guest goes right. They greet each other and proceed as in Part One.

XU XIAN:

Now, reverend sir, for what purpose have you deigned to call on me?

FA HAI:

I'm here about an ailment.

XU XIAN [*rising*]:
An ailment? Then allow me to call on my wife to see you.

FA HAI:
Ha!

XU XIAN:
Why do you laugh, sir?

FA HAI:
Because it is not I who am sick, but you. It is I who have come to treat you.

XU XIAN:
But sir, as you can see, I am in robust health. I suffer from no illness.

FA HAI:
Not only you, but this whole shop is enveloped in an overwhelming miasma of sorcery. I could sense it miles away. Then, look at you—your face is an abnormal color—a sign of deep-seated poison. Intercession prayers must begin immediately.

XU XIAN:
Oh, I see. And are these intercession prayers in exchange for some donation perhaps?

FA HAI:
Don't insult me.

XU XIAN:
Well then, surely you're joking. This is a respectable neighborhood, not a whiff of evil sorcery here. And even if there were, my wife is a skilled herbalist. So you see, I'm in no danger at all.

FA HAI:

Master Xu, your wife is not an herbalist.

XU XIAN:

Indeed she is!

FA HAI:

She is not even a human being.

XU XIAN:

What?

FA HAI:

She is a demon spirit, sir, a snake who has managed to transform herself through sorcery into the form of a woman. Right now she's coiled up somewhere near—I sense it. She slithered down the mountainside, to which she rightly belongs, right into your shop.

[*Pause.*]

XU XIAN:

I'm speechless.

FA HAI:

Get rid of her at once or she'll destroy you.

XU XIAN:

Reverend, I must ask you to curtail this nonsense immediately. My wife is the most virtuous of women. I've never met anyone so loving, so kind.

FA HAI:
That's all a trick.

XU XIAN:
Oh? And her serving the poor and the sick, that's all a trick too?

FA HAI:
Listen to me, son, that thing in your bedroom is not human—and one day you'll die at her hands.

XU XIAN:
Really? Snakes don't have hands.

FA HAI:
All right then. It's only because you are of a good family I tried to warn you. But if you won't listen to reason—

XU XIAN:
Reason? My wife's a snake? That's reason?

FA HAI:
If you won't listen to reason, there's no hope for you. I'll be on my way.

[FA HAI *begins to exit.*]

XU XIAN:
Yes!

[FA HAI *turns back. Ominous music begins.*]

FA HAI:
Only do this for me. On the day of the Dragon Boat Festival, serve your wife a cup of realgar wine.

XU XIAN:
What on earth for?

FA HAI:
You know what for. On that day, when they drink the wine, all creatures reveal their true form.

XU XIAN:
Yeah, I'll keep that in mind.

FA HAI:
Do as I say and watch what happens.

XU XIAN:
Yes, thank you. Good-bye.

FA HAI:
Amithabha Buddha!

[FA HAI *exits. Music ends.* XU XIAN *sits in one of the chairs.*]

NARRATOR FIVE:
Xu Xian did not bother to see him off. He sat alone in the guest room.

XU XIAN:
Preposterous.

NARRATOR FIVE:
But still, he felt uneasy. He began to be tormented by that old doubt.

[DOUBT *enters and begins to pick at* XU XIAN *with her long fingernails.*]

XU XIAN:
Nonsense.

[XU XIAN *rises from his chair and heads toward the cabinet.*]

NARRATOR FIVE:
Nonetheless, he made his way upstairs to where Bai Suzhen was sleeping.

[XU XIAN *opens the cabinet. Sweet music.*]

He gazed down on her in her bed. She looked so beautiful, so kind and peaceful: there was not a thing about her that was not perfectly good. His doubt had slipped away.

[DOUBT *exits.* XU XIAN *laughs.*]

WHITE SNAKE [*waking*]:
Why are you laughing, my love?

XU XIAN:
Oh, I was only thinking how soon I'll be the father of a fat little baby in this house.

WHITE SNAKE:
You're more like the baby, to laugh at that.

THE DRAGON BOAT FESTIVAL

[*Music.* XU XIAN *helps* WHITE SNAKE *out of the cabinet and closes its doors.*]

NARRATOR FIVE:
The days flew by, and the Dragon Boat Festival approached. Everyone was busy making special dumplings and putting up decorations and good luck charms. The shop was especially thronged.

[*Music swells. The cabinet sinks to counter level.* XU XIAN, WHITE SNAKE, *and* GREEN SNAKE *try to decorate the cabinet with strings of paper dumplings but are soon interrupted by the arrival of customers who fill the shop, each bringing a long list for the pharmacy and perhaps a gift for* WHITE SNAKE. GREEN SNAKE *runs around trying to fill orders. Everything is very busy. The audience cannot really hear individual voices, but the customers might say the following.*]

CUSTOMER ONE:
Master Xu, here's my list: ginseng, mushrooms, wolfberry, Dang Gui, Astragalus, Atractylodes—

CUSTOMER TWO:
And mine—I need Bupleurum, Coptis chinensis, ginger—

CUSTOMER THREE:
And mine as well—licorice, ephedra, peony, rehmannia, rhubarb, salvia—

CUSTOMER FOUR:
Lady Bai, would you accept these cakes in appreciation for all you've done this year?

CUSTOMER FIVE [*with gifts*]:
Lady Bai, Lady Bai . . .

WHITE SNAKE:
Why thank you, too kind—

CUSTOMER FOUR:
And here's my list as well . . .

WHITE SNAKE [*audibly, above the fray*]:
Greenie, I need six ounces of tamarind root—it's in the back!

[GREEN SNAKE *starts to go but suddenly is seized with serpentine convulsions. A large, long snake tail drops from beneath her tunic. She desperately hides it. Music fades.*]

GREEN SNAKE:
Yes, missssssssssss—

[GREEN SNAKE *can't stop the letter "s." She writhes on the ground. The customers slowly notice.*]

WHITE SNAKE:
Greenie!

GREEN SNAKE:
tressssssssssssssss—

XU XIAN:
What's the matter with her?

[GREEN SNAKE *continues to hiss. The customers stare in silence.*]

WHITE SNAKE:

Nothing, I'm sure she's just tired. Let me have a look at her, if you can hold down the shop.

[WHITE SNAKE *dashes over to* GREEN SNAKE, *who can't control her movements on the floor. The customers gradually leave the shop.* XU XIAN *cleans behind the counter.*]

GREEN SNAKE:

Dear friend, I can't hold out much longer! Even up on the mountainssssssside, when the dragon boatssss went by—even at that distansssssse—we reverted to our original shape!

WHITE SNAKE:

I know it. I know. Listen: I think I can hold out, I have many centuries' more practice than you, but look at you—I'm worried.

GREEN SNAKE:

Let'ssssss flee together right away and hide in the meadows until thiss damned fessstival is over!

WHITE SNAKE:

I can't leave.

GREEN SNAKE:

You mussssss—you have to! It was an inconveniensssse when we changed up there, but down here?

WHITE SNAKE:

I can't leave my husband's side—he'll grow suspicious. And besides, I love him so, I don't want to leave even for a minute.

GREEN SNAKE:
What shall we do?

WHITE SNAKE:
You have to go away alone.

GREEN SNAKE:
No!

WHITE SNAKE:
Fly straightaway to some shady grove far away and stay there—at least until after midday tomorrow.

XU XIAN:
How are things going? Greenie, are you all right?

WHITE SNAKE:
No, she's not—but it's nothing a little rest won't cure. Greenie, go upstairs and stay in your room until tomorrow afternoon.

XU XIAN:
But she'll miss the festival. And we're drowning here.

WHITE SNAKE:
It can't be helped.

GREEN SNAKE:
I don't want to go alone.

WHITE SNAKE:
Don't be silly, you know the way to your room.

GREEN SNAKE:
I don't want to go.

WHITE SNAKE:
Greenie!

[GREEN SNAKE *exits.*]

XU XIAN:
For all her nonsense, she is devoted.

WHITE SNAKE:
Yesssssssss.

[WHITE SNAKE *quickly covers her mouth.*]

[*Very lively drumming and music: the Dragon Boat Festival. The cabinet sinks into the floor. Celebrants enter from all over, all of them drinking and in different states of inebriation. Several small dragon boats are pulled by on strings. We see puppet* GREEN SNAKE *glide by and hide in some bamboo.* XU XIAN *and* WHITE SNAKE *come strolling on, arm in arm.* XU XIAN *is carrying a small jug of realgar wine. He is tipsy.*]

XU XIAN:
I can't recall there was ever a more perfect day for the festival. Not a cloud in the sky, and yet such breezes.

WHITE SNAKE:
Yes.

XU XIAN [*playfully quoting Qu Yuan*]:
"Nine fields of orchids at one time I grew,
For sweet clover, a hundred acres too,
And fifty acres for the azaleas bright,
The rumex fragrant and the lichen white . . ."

WHITE SNAKE [*applauding*]:
Very good! You studied hard—do you regret you are not a scholar?

XU XIAN:
I regret not one thing, not one breath, not one step that might have altered the path of my life by one meter and prevented me from arriving here at this spot, with you by my side, at this moment.

[*They sit and rest. The music continues "in the distance."*]

WHITE SNAKE:
My dear, I'm feeling a little tired. It is very hot, after all.

XU XIAN:
Here, have some wine, it will revive you.

WHITE SNAKE:
No, thank you.

XU XIAN:
Yes, it's good for you and you haven't drunk yet—everyone must drink today.

WHITE SNAKE:
I don't care to!

XU XIAN:
What? On the day of the dragon boats? You're like Qu Yuan him-self, "All the world is drunk, while I alone am sober. So I am dismissed!"

WHITE SNAKE:
Oh, please.

XU XIAN [*offering the wine*]:
Here you go.

WHITE SNAKE:
No—think of the baby.

XU XIAN:
A little won't hurt.

[XU XIAN *laughs.*]

WHITE SNAKE:
What is it?

XU XIAN:
I wasn't going to tell you, but . . . someone came by the other day. Actually, a well-known monk: Fa Hai of Golden Mountain.

WHITE SNAKE [*alarmed*]:
Fa Hai?

XU XIAN:
He has a big reputation, but . . .

[xu xian *laughs again.*]

WHITE SNAKE:
What? But what?

XU XIAN:
He told me to make sure you drank realgar wine today because . . .
[*laughing*]

WHITE SNAKE:
Because?

XU XIAN:
Because you're a demon! [*Laughing drunkenly*] A terrible, terrible
demon!

WHITE SNAKE:
Oh, he did, did he?

XU XIAN:
He said that if you drank the wine you could not help but resume
your "original" shape.

[xu xian *makes the gesture of a snake crawling with his hand.* WHITE
SNAKE *reaches for the jug.*]

WHITE SNAKE:
Give me that.

XU XIAN:
You needn't—

WHITE SNAKE:
Give me that.

[WHITE SNAKE *drinks.*]

Now, take me home. I'm tired and . . . feeling ill.

[*Music: a strange, distorted sound.* XU XIAN *leads* WHITE SNAKE *back home, back to her bedroom.*]

NARRATOR FIVE:
Xu Xian immediately felt ashamed that he had pushed the wine on his beloved wife. They hurried home, where she retired to her chamber.

XU XIAN:
Shall I get you anything?

WHITE SNAKE:
No, no. I'll be fine, just . . . leave me be. Let me rest.

[WHITE SNAKE *closes herself in the cabinet.*]

XU XIAN:
I'm mortified. I should never have pressed the wine on her in her condition. Darling? You know your own cure best—what should I do? What concoction should I make up?

WHITE SNAKE [*from inside cabinet*]:
Nothing—nothing at all. Just . . . leave me. Ooooooooooh!

XU XIAN:
What's the matter! Oh, what's the matter?

WHITE SNAKE [*groaning in pain*]:
Oh! Oooooh!

XU XIAN:
My love!

[XU XIAN *opens the cabinet. There is a huge, writhing white snake inside. A wild cacophony of cymbals and hissing.* XU XIAN *backs away and appears to faint.* NARRATOR FIVE *comes forward and closes the doors. The music is sad.*]

NARRATOR FIVE:
No one should see what Xu Xian saw. It struck him dumb with terror. His blood froze and his heart stopped dead. And his little soul fled—forever?

[*On the word "fled"* NARRATOR FIVE *reaches into* XU XIAN*'s tunic and pulls out a little piece of gold material. As he draws it away,* XU XIAN *reaches for it, but he cannot retrieve it.* NARRATOR FIVE *exits with* XU XIAN*'s soul. Music ends.*]

GREEN SNAKE [*entering, in human form*]:
Master Xu, Lady Bai! I'm feeling all better. I went out for a walk and—

[GREEN SNAKE *sees* XU XIAN *and rushes to him.*]
Master Xu? Master Xu? What has happened? Lady Bai?!

[*Inside the cabinet,* WHITE SNAKE *groans faintly.* GREEN SNAKE *opens the cabinet.* WHITE SNAKE *tumbles out in human form.*]

Mistress!

WHITE SNAKE:

Oh, Greenie, it's terrible. I drank the wine—I thought I could hold out but I couldn't. Oh, I pray Master Xu didn't see me.

GREEN SNAKE:

I believe he may have.

WHITE SNAKE:

He did? Greenie, where did he go? Has he left me?

GREEN SNAKE:

In a manner of speaking . . .

WHITE SNAKE:

What do you mean?

GREEN SNAKE:

He's just over there—but, Lady Bai, I fear he is dead.

WHITE SNAKE [*running to* XU XIAN]:

Oh my love, my heart is breaking! Come back, come back. Greenie, help me!

GREEN SNAKE:

Dear friend, don't dissolve, don't lose your mind!

WHITE SNAKE:

Oh, what can I do?

GREEN SNAKE:

Think! Is there no herb, no potion we have that can restore life?

WHITE SNAKE:
No, there's nothing . . . except . . .

GREEN SNAKE:
What is it?

WHITE SNAKE:
The glossy ganoderma plant—

GREEN SNAKE:
Oh, mistress, that's all the way to the Kunlun Forest—

WHITE SNAKE:
I know.

GREEN SNAKE:
—and they say there's only one. And it's guarded too! By the Crane and the Stag Spirit! You could lose your life!

WHITE SNAKE:
What is my life, now that I've cost Xu Xian his?

GREEN SNAKE:
Don't talk that way!

WHITE SNAKE:
I'm going. Stay here and hide Master Xu. Say that he is ill. If I'm not back in three days' time, then I am not returning. Then bury him and return to our mountain.

[WHITE SNAKE *runs off.*]

GREEN SNAKE:
Lady Bai!

THE KUNLUN FOREST

[*Night. Drumming. Many members of the company come forward. They chant individually and together.*]

SOLO VOICE:
The air is cold and the night is black—

ALL:
Fly through it all, Lady Bai!

SOLO VOICE:
The rivers are wide and the mountain high—

ALL:
Don't be afraid, Lady Bai!

SOLO VOICE:
Far below is the emerald sea,

SEVERAL VOICES:
So far so far from the pharmacy;

MORE VOICES:
If your heart stops now then so will he—

ALL:
But your heart never stops, Lady Bai!

[*The Kunlun Forest descends from above. Dozens of bamboo poles.* WHITE SNAKE *enters in puppet form, slithering around the company and the bamboo.*]

SOLO VOICE:
The Kunlun Forest is dark and deep—

ALL:
Crawl through the moss, Lady Bai!

SOLO VOICE:
Watch out now, the path is steep—

ALL:
Don't make a hiss, Lady Bai!

SOLO VOICE:
There, right there, the ganoderma glows—

SEVERAL VOICES:
Hurry oh hurry his heart grows cold—

MORE VOICES:
Lost in the world is a lonely soul—

ALL:
Let your heart never stop, Lady Bai!

[*The company rises and begins to retreat.*]

ALL:
Love comes like lightning and falls like rain.
What can you do, Lady Bai?

One part pleasure and two parts pain.
Go! Go! Go! Lady Bai!

[*Company departs.* WHITE SNAKE *is about to steal the ganoderma herb when the* STAG SPIRIT *rises up to confront her.*]

STAG SPIRIT:
You there! You little demon, what do you think you are doing?!

WHITE SNAKE:
Oh, you frightened me—

STAG SPIRIT:
What are you doing in this sacred grove?

WHITE SNAKE:
I came for the ganoderma herb—

STAG SPIRIT:
Stealing our herbs?

WHITE SNAKE:
I don't want to steal it, but there was no one to ask—I didn't want to disturb you as you slept.

STAG SPIRIT:
Ha! This grove and everything in it belongs to Canopus, the Immortal of the South Pole, and Crane and I are his guards.

WHITE SNAKE:
Listen to me: my husband—

STAG SPIRIT:
Husband?

WHITE SNAKE:
My mortal husband has died. I just need one petal of the glossy gan-oderma to revive him—just this one. Nothing like this grows on earth. I know that Canopus would have compassion if he were to hear me. You've heard it yourself—"In the eyes of Heaven it is bet-ter to save one man's life than to build a seven-story pagoda."

STAG SPIRIT:
It is irregular.

WHITE SNAKE:
I know, I know. But I've come so far and if I don't hurry back this minute it will be too late.

STAG SPIRIT:
Hmmmm . . . all right, then. One petal, this one time. But you had better hurry along out of here before Brother Crane gets back.

WHITE SNAKE:
I thank you one thousand times—

[WHITE SNAKE *begins to leave but is stopped by the* CRANE SPIRIT, *who raises its terrifying wings.*]

CRANE SPIRIT:
Where do you think you're going?! That herb is for immortals not little snake spirits!

STAG SPIRIT:

Brother Crane! What are you doing here? You are meant to accompany the Immortal to the Western Heaven and listen to him expound on the classics!

CRANE SPIRIT:

I was there, but I sensed something was up. I've never had snake meat before, I'm looking forward to it.

[CRANE SPIRIT *holds* WHITE SNAKE *down with its beak.*]

STAG SPIRIT:

Brother Crane—

[CANOPUS *enters. He is very tall, bald, and carries a long staff.*]

CANOPUS:

Brother Crane, cease this instant! This violence is intolerable!

CRANE SPIRIT:

Venerable Immortal, this little demon is thieving from your grotto. Let me devour her!

CANOPUS:

Absolutely not. I know very well what the White Snake is doing. I expected she would come this evening, which is why I asked you to accompany me to the meeting in the Western Heaven, Brother Crane, and let the Stag Spirit guard tonight. He is far more gentle than you.

[STAG SPIRIT *is well pleased with this compliment.*]

CRANE SPIRIT:
That herb is for immortals only—

CANOPUS:
We will make an exception this once.

CRANE SPIRIT [*reluctant*]:
I will obey.

[CRANE SPIRIT *releases* WHITE SNAKE, *who curls up close to* CANOPUS.]

CANOPUS:
It is not the White Snake's fate to be swallowed up by a Crane. Now run along, little snake, don't be afraid. And you two, follow me.

[CANOPUS *strides off.*]

CRANE SPIRIT [*to* WHITE SNAKE]:
Creep on out of here, then, but remember: You'll never be immortal and you'll never be human either.

STAG SPIRIT:
Brother Crane!

CRANE SPIRIT:
You come all this way, fly all this distance, risk your life—and for what? You think your beloved husband would do the same for you if he could see you as you really are? No mortal can see you in your true form and not be repulsed. You think he'd go to the ends of the earth for you? He wouldn't go to the end of the street!

[*Drums. All depart. The forest of bamboo rises out of sight.*]

WAKING XU XIAN

[*In the transition a large cloud silk comes over* WHITE SNAKE *from upstage, and when it curls back up toward her and off, it reveals her in her human form with the herb in her mouth. Simultaneously, a smaller linen cloth is carried on downstage, held like a curtain between two performers. It travels upstage, hiding the action behind it. When released, it covers the body of* XU XIAN, *laid out on the bed—which is the cabinet raised to a level of one foot.* GREEN SNAKE *is there.*]

GREEN SNAKE:
Mistress, you're back! Oh, thank heavens—do you have it? Did you get the herb?

WHITE SNAKE [*distracted, only looking at* XU XIAN]:
Yes, it's here.

GREEN SNAKE:
Oh, my heavens! And will it work?

WHITE SNAKE:
Yes, I'm sure it will. Take it.

GREEN SNAKE:
You're sure?

WHITE SNAKE:
Yes, yes, make the preparation.

[GREEN SNAKE *runs off with the herb. She continues the conversation from offstage.* WHITE SNAKE *goes to* XU XIAN. *All of her attention is on him.*]

GREEN SNAKE:
Oh, mistress, I've missed you so much. I had to close up the shop and say you both were ill [*returns, crushing the herb with mortar and pestle*] and there were visitors all the time and Madame Lin came and—but what am I saying? What about you? How was it? Did you meet the Stag Spirit?

WHITE SNAKE:
Yes.

GREEN SNAKE:
And the Crane?

WHITE SNAKE:
Yes, I met him as well.

GREEN SNAKE:
And did you persuade them? Or was there an enormous battle? Oh, what I wouldn't give to have seen it!

WHITE SNAKE:
It was nothing glorious.

GREEN SNAKE:
How can you say that? Traveling all that way and . . . anyway, you'll tell me all about it, but here [*offering the herb*]—

WHITE SNAKE:
Greenie, hold on a moment.

GREEN SNAKE:
Yes?

WHITE SNAKE:
Before we give this potion, we need to think. We need a plan. When Xu Xian wakes up, he may remember what he saw. What on earth will we say?

GREEN SNAKE:
I've had three days to think of that. I know my powers don't compare with yours, but I can conjure up a thing or two myself, you'll see—I have a trick—just play along. It won't be hard, I promise you. How soon will Master Xu wake up after the potion?

WHITE SNAKE:
He should revive right away but he won't be conscious for hours. Oh, Greenie, I'm exhausted.

GREEN SNAKE:
All right then—just call me for tea when he wakes, that will be the sign. Now here it is, let's go.

[WHITE SNAKE *hesitates.*]

What's the matter?

WHITE SNAKE:
He saw me, as I really am. They have a saying, "Seeing is believing."

GREEN SNAKE:

No, no. Not with these humans—you have it wrong: "Believing is seeing." You'll see. Now, come on.

[WHITE SNAKE *gives the potion. A shimmering sound.* XU XIAN's *soul falls from the sky.* WHITE SNAKE *catches it and puts it in his chest. With a great gasp he revives but then sinks back down and turns over to sleep.*]

WHITE SNAKE:

It's a kind of miracle, I suppose.

GREEN SNAKE:

No, my lady, it is you who are the miracle. Now, you go to sleep while I practice my trick.

[WHITE SNAKE *crawls into bed with* XU XIAN *and falls asleep.* GREEN SNAKE *takes her white sash, waves it in the air, then lets it fly.*]

Abraca-snakie!

[*Nothing happens. She tries again.*]

Crawla-coleebra!

[*Nothing happens. She throws the sash offstage.*]

Serpentino!

[*Something happens.* GREEN SNAKE *appears to follow something off-stage, trying to catch it. Now it is morning. The sound of birds.* XU XIAN *wakes up, drowsy, relaxed. He looks around sleepily. Suddenly he sees* WHITE SNAKE *lying beside him. He screams and tears out of the bed, taking the cover with him, to huddle against the wall.*]

WHITE SNAKE:
My love, what is the matter? Have you had a nightmare? Whatever is the matter?

XU XIAN [*accusing, terrified*]:
You know!

WHITE SNAKE:
No, I don't. I—

XU XIAN:
Stop! Stop right there!

WHITE SNAKE:
Whatever—?

XU XIAN:
Don't come near me! He was right about you!

WHITE SNAKE [*secretly panicked*]:
Greenie, Greenie!

[GREEN SNAKE *enters.*]

Could you bring us some tea? Master Xu is awake.

XU XIAN:
I am! I am awake!—

GREEN SNAKE:
Right away, madam.

[GREEN SNAKE *exits, pausing slightly to cast spell toward offstage.*]

XU XIAN:
I see what you are!—

WHITE SNAKE:
You've been ill for three days . . .

GREEN SNAKE [*running on*]:
EEEEEK! EEEEEEEK!

WHITE SNAKE:
Greenie?

GREEN SNAKE:
It's in the courtyard, madam!

WHITE SNAKE:
What is in the courtyard?

XU XIAN [*in a panic*]:
Yes, what?!!

GREEN SNAKE:
That same horrible white snake you saw on the day of the Dragon Boat Festival!

WHITE SNAKE:
Oh no!

GREEN SNAKE:
Oh! It is coming in here. Oh, EEEEKK!

[*A performer enters with a white snake puppet slithering rapidly.* WHITE SNAKE *catches on immediately. Havoc. The false serpent wildly chases the ladies and threatens the terrified* XU XIAN.]

GREEN SNAKE AND WHITE SNAKE:
EEEEEK—

WHITE SNAKE:
I HATE SNAKES!!

GREEN SNAKE:
ME TOO. OOOOOHHHH!

[*The ladies jump onto the bed and cling to each other in exaggerated girlish terror.*]

WHITE SNAKE:
Xu Xian, save us!

GREEN SNAKE:
Kill it for us, Master Xu!

WHITE SNAKE:
Ladies hate snakes!

GREEN SNAKE:
Please, Master Xu! EEEEEEEEK!

WHITE SNAKE:
EEEEEEEEKKKKK!

[XU XIAN, *with great horror, grabs the puppet out of the performer's hand and hurls it against the wall. It clatters to the floor.* XU XIAN *is stupefied.*]

GREEN SNAKE:
Thank you, Master Xu!

WHITE SNAKE:
Oh, thank you! Thank goodness you were here!

GREEN SNAKE [*going to the dead snake*]:
Do you see, madam, surely it's the same—

WHITE SNAKE:
The same one—

GREEN SNAKE:
The same one that was in your bed—

WHITE SNAKE:
On the day of the festival—

GREEN SNAKE:
That caused you to groan and cry out—

WHITE SNAKE:
Oh yes!

GREEN SNAKE:
I heard you groaning even from my room—

WHITE SNAKE:
Yes!

GREEN SNAKE:
And then I came in and Master Xu was passed out cold.

WHITE SNAKE:
You were so startled.

GREEN SNAKE:
But look at him now, he's cured, and overcome his fear.

WHITE SNAKE:
And that snake won't bother us anymore.

GREEN SNAKE [*bowing deeply*]:
Thank you, Master Xu.

[*Pause.*]

XU XIAN:
But . . .

WHITE SNAKE:
Yes?

XU XIAN:
But the snake I saw that day was . . . was bigger.

WHITE SNAKE [*sympathetically*]:
Nooooo.

XU XIAN:
Much, much—

WHITE SNAKE:
     I don't think so—

XU XIAN:
          Much bigger.

WHITE SNAKE [*sidewinding up to him*]:
Oh, darling, you were drunk.

GREEN SNAKE [*laughing*]:
Yes—drunk Master Xu! I'll say!

WHITE SNAKE:
Remember?

XU XIAN:
It's true I'd had some drinks, but I mean it was *much* . . .

WHITE SNAKE:
And besides,

XU XIAN:
     Much . . .

WHITE SNAKE:
remember that nonsense that old monk put in your head?

XU XIAN:
       Much bigger . . .

GREEN SNAKE [*genuinely taken aback*]:
What nonsense is that, my lady? What monk?

WHITE SNAKE [*sitting with* XU XIAN *on the bed*]:
Oh, that old Fa Hai has been spreading rumors that I was a demon spirit or something. That was in your head—and remember what they say: believing is seeing . . .

GREEN SNAKE:
Fa Hai?

XU XIAN:
I confess, I couldn't help but think of what he'd said . . .

GREEN SNAKE:
What? That bald-headed ass who was in the shop the other day? He told you my lady is a demon spirit? How could you ever, Master Xu! I saw in a moment he was no good! You should know, my Lady Bai was up day and night nursing you back to health. You were half-dead! No—you *were* dead! And only she in all the world had the skill to save you. She risked her own health, her own life, in fact—

[GREEN SNAKE *is about to reveal too much.*]

WHITE SNAKE:
Greenie!

GREEN SNAKE:
You have no idea!

WHITE SNAKE:
Greenie!

[WHITE SNAKE *looks at her significantly.* GREEN SNAKE *sulks off.*]

XU XIAN:
I feel very tired.

WHITE SNAKE:
You're not quite recovered, my dear. Listen to me. Swear to me that you will never have anything to do with that old monk again.

XU XIAN [*persuaded*]:
I won't. I won't.

WHITE SNAKE:
You see what harm he has caused already.

[WHITE SNAKE *fetches the bed cover that is lying across the room.*]

XU XIAN:
I do.

WHITE SNAKE:
Who knows what he could do in the future?

XU XIAN:
Oh, I swear.

WHITE SNAKE:
Now come lie down.

XU XIAN:
Oh, thank heavens! I feel I've awakened from the longest nightmare!

WHITE SNAKE [*as she eases him back to bed*]:
You have, my love, you have.

XU XIAN:
And now I'm back—back to the real world.

WHITE SNAKE:
Yes, you are.

[*He sleeps. She sighs and looks skyward.*]

FA HAI LURES XU XIAN

[*Music.* NARRATOR TWO *enters. As he speaks,* XU XIAN *and* WHITE SNAKE *rise and fold the bed cover. The cabinet sinks level to the ground. They kiss good-bye, and* XU XIAN *goes walking as* WHITE SNAKE *exits.*]

NARRATOR TWO:
Life soon returned to normal at the Bao He Pharmacy. The experiences of the day of the Dragon Boat Festival fell away from Xu Xian's mind, and the days of summer slipped by like a fish through a stream. Soon, the air was clean, and the blue sky was sharp against the yellow leaves of autumn. Then, one day, Xu Xian went to settle an account with a client. On his way home he was wandering by the river, when—

[*Music fades.* FA HAI *is suddenly following* XU XIAN.]

FA HAI [*humbly calling out*]:
Oh, Master Xu!

XU XIAN:

Sir Abbott, hello. Forgive me, but I've no time to visit, I must be getting home.

FA HAI:

Just one word—

XU XIAN:

     I'm so sorry, I really have no time . . .

FA HAI:

          —In the name of Buddha!

XU XIAN:

Very well.

FA HAI:

Might I inquire, what happened the day of the Dragon Boat Festival?

XU XIAN:

Why nothing. Not one thing. Nothing at all. It was a very nice festival.

FA HAI:

Your esteemed wife drank the wine?

XU XIAN:

She did, as a matter of fact.

FA HAI:

And?

XU XIAN:
And she was absolutely fine.

FA HAI:
I thought so.

XU XIAN:
What?

FA HAI:
Well, it's always best to take precautions. When I returned to the monastery the night we met, I redid my calculations and I saw I'd made an error. The White Snake reincarnation isn't due for another century. So there was nothing to my suspicions after all.

XU XIAN:
Well, really—you might have let me know.

FA HAI:
Forgive an old man, Master Xu. And let me make amends.

XU XIAN:
It isn't necessary.

FA HAI:
I insist.

XU XIAN:
I should be going.

[*Music.*]

FA HAI [*wrapping his arm over* XU XIAN's *shoulder*]:
The view of the autumn leaves from Golden Monastery is something to behold, Master Xu. How long has it been since you've been up to visit us?

XU XIAN:
It's been quite some time, I confess.

FA HAI:
Why not come with me now? Let's go up the mountain. We'll burn incense together and then have tea upon the terrace and compose a few verses on the view. I've heard you're fond of poetry.

XU XIAN [*very flattered*]:
Why, yes I am. I accept your invitation. But I can't stay long.

FA HAI:
No, no. We'll go on up the mountain and you'll come right back down again by end of day.

XU XIAN:
All right then.

[*As the narration continues,* XU XIAN *and* FA HAI *board a boat and travel in the same manner that* XU XIAN *and the ladies traveled when they met. The music of that scene is reprised, in a minor key.*]

NARRATOR TWO:
Xu Xian and Fa Hai strolled together along the banks of the river, then took a boat to the other side, all the while expounding verses and sometimes quoting scripture. Xu Xian felt flattered by the attentions of such a high-ranking monk. They climbed up the mountain, and at last they entered the gates of the Golden Monastery.

[*The* BOATMAN *holds his pole up high and horizontal to become the gate of the monastery.* XU XIAN *and* FA HAI *enter underneath. An* ACOLYTE *is there. Throughout the scene the monastery bell rings as before, slow and ponderous.*]

FA HAI:
Please, prepare some vegetarian dishes for our guest.

[*The* ACOLYTE *departs.*]

XU XIAN:
Sir Abbot, you really shouldn't go to all this trouble just for me. I can't stay—

[XU XIAN *catches sight of the view. As he goes to look,* FA HAI *shuts the gate by pushing the pole down. Then the* BOATMAN *exits with the pole.*]

Oh my, that certainly is a view: "the autumn leaves are touched by rays of"—

FA HAI:
Sir, you're married to a snake.

[XU XIAN *is completely bewildered.*]

You are coiled in the snares of a snake demon.

XU XIAN:
What are you talking about? You said you miscalculated!

FA HAI:
And that servant of hers—that Green thing?

XU XIAN:
You mean Greenie?

FA HAI:
Snake.

XU XIAN:
This is preposterous. I advise you, sir, to stop slandering virtuous young women.

FA HAI:
They are neither virtuous, nor young, nor women. They are snake spirits that have spent hundreds of years cultivating their magic powers. You remember the theft of gold ingots from the Magistrate's last spring? That green thing was behind it—it's how you built your shop! With stolen money! And the two of them conspired to fool you after the festival. It was indeed your wife you discovered hissing in your sheets, but the green one conjured up a third snake to fool you.

XU XIAN:
I'm going.

FA HAI:
Your only hope is to convert.

XU XIAN:
Convert?

FA HAI:

It is the only way to protect yourself.

XU XIAN:

What?! Is that what this is about? You want me to become a monk? You want me to abandon my home and family?

FA HAI:

Your "family" is an unnatural alliance. It's nothing but a nest of vipers. If you do not leave them they shall soon be deprived of you in any case, for they will eat you.

XU XIAN:

Well, I'm very grateful for your concern on my behalf, but I have no intention of leaving my family. I choose to stay in this vale of tears. If, indeed, my wife—who is at this moment serving customers in our pharmacy and wondering where I am—if she is a snake demon I am confident I can avoid her snares by myself. It is getting late and I must go now.

FA HAI:

I'm afraid that won't be possible. The gates of the mountain are locked tight. You cannot leave.

[FA HAI *signals for the* ACOLYTE, *who comes to take* XU XIAN *off. They exit. Transitional music.*]

WHERE IS HE?

[*Back at the shop. The cabinet is up to counter height. In this scene, several feet of the tails of both* WHITE SNAKE *and* GREEN SNAKE *are showing beneath their robes.* WHITE SNAKE *is heavily pregnant and frantic.*]

WHITE SNAKE:
But where can he have got to? All this time—and no message?

GREEN SNAKE:
You have to calm down, mistress. I'm sure—

WHITE SNAKE:
I can't hold out much long—[*hears something*] What's that—?

GREEN SNAKE:
What?

WHITE SNAKE:
On the stair, do you hear? Go! Go!

[GREEN SNAKE *exits.*]

Is it him?

GREEN SNAKE [*returning*]:
It's only the cat come home.

WHITE SNAKE:
Oh, where is he?

[MADAME LIN *approaches the shop.*]

GREEN SNAKE:
Perhaps when he'd settled the account, the customer detained him and they drank too much wine and can't—oh! It's Madame Lin.

[*They both kick their tails behind them.* WHITE SNAKE *backs up to behind the counter.* GREEN SNAKE *joins her.*]

WHITE SNAKE:
Good day, Madame Lin.

MADAME LIN:
Good day, Lady Bai.

GREEN SNAKE:
What may we do for you today?

MADAME LIN:
I'm out of my Dang Gui.

GREEN SNAKE:
Three ounces?

[GREEN SNAKE *reaches under the counter for a jar and begins to measure out and wrap.*]

MADAME LIN:
Yes, that's right. Is Master Xu around? I wanted to—

WHITE SNAKE:
He went to settle an account with a client.

MADAME LIN:
Oh, is the monastery now taking herbs?

WHITE SNAKE:
Is the what?

MADAME LIN:
Is the monastery now subscribing?

WHITE SNAKE:
Why, not that I know of. Why do you say that?

MADAME LIN:
Oh, no reason. It's just that I saw Master Xu walking with Abbott Fa Hai the other day, I thought perhaps that was the client you meant.

[*Everything stops. A pause.*]

WHITE SNAKE [*slowly, a sort of question*]:
No—?

MADAME LIN:
They seemed very intent on their conversation. Has Master Xu become interested in religious instruction? You should warn him, the Abbot is very enlightened of course, but he has a strong, how shall I say—

GREEN SNAKE:
Odor?

MADAME LIN:
I was going to say *personality.* But now that you mention—

WHITE SNAKE:
I'm afraid we're closing early.

[*Coming forward and hustling* MADAME LIN *out of the shop.*]

MADAME LIN:
Oh, you are?

WHITE SNAKE:
Yes, pardon me. We're closing early today.

MADAME LIN:
I'll be on my way then.

WHITE SNAKE:
Yes, thank you.

[MADAME LIN *exits.* WHITE SNAKE *is furious.*]

Fa Hai? How could I not have seen it! And yet, how is it possible? Xu Xian swore a solemn oath to me! He said he would never listen to that old monk again—how could he deceive me!

GREEN SNAKE:
Oh, madam, people make vows all the time and then just forget them! That's just what they do. Besides, that old monk is so crafty, and the master is so—well, he's easily persuaded.

WHITE SNAKE:
Just because he's so sincere, don't make fun of him. It's a virtue!

GREEN SNAKE:
I'm not making fun—

WHITE SNAKE:
Oh why is that atrocious monk so bent on meddling in my affairs? Why does he want to destroy my happy marriage? What's it to him?

GREEN SNAKE:

Who knows? In any case, I think it's time we leave this dusty world and go back to our mountain and live in peace.

WHITE SNAKE:

Easy for you to say! I'm expecting a baby—and I love Xu Xian.

GREEN SNAKE:

But, madam, why?

WHITE SNAKE:

There is no why!

GREEN SNAKE:

You're risking too much, and . . .

WHITE SNAKE:

We're going up there.

GREEN SNAKE:

What?

WHITE SNAKE:

You heard me. We're going up to that monastery. Xu Xian has been kidnapped.

GREEN SNAKE:

I don't know if that's a good idea, my lady; maybe Master Xu wasn't kidnapped, after all. Maybe—

WHITE SNAKE [*leaving*]:

Are you coming?

[GREEN SNAKE *runs after* WHITE SNAKE. *The cabinet sinks to stage level.*]

ACOLYTES

[*Back at the monastery. The temple bell rings throughout the scene as before.* XU XIAN *and the* ACOLYTE *are sitting. The* ACOLYTE *is always very calm. In front of them is a bowl filled with pointy dried twigs.*]

ACOLYTE:
Please try to eat something, Brother Xu. At the monastery we only have these vegetarian dishes. They are strange at first but you will get used to them.

XU XIAN [*barely containing himself*]:
I am perfectly used to vegetarian dishes—I'm not eating anything because I'm sick at heart!

ACOLYTE:
I understand. When one first decides to join the Buddhist brotherhood things can be hard. But soon—

XU XIAN:
I did not decide to join the Buddhist brotherhood! I came here to look at the view! I was tricked by Fa Hai!

ACOLYTE:
You did not come to become a monk?

XU XIAN:
No!

ACOLYTE:

But the Abbott said you were his new disciple. He said you were haunted by a demon and came here to take holy orders. Don't worry, Brother Xu, Fa Hai can exorcise any demon—

XU XIAN:

No, no no! There isn't any—oh my god, do those bells never stop!?!!—There isn't any demon! Fa Hai is lying through his teeth! You've got to get me out of here!

ACOLYTE:

Come, come, Brother Xu—

XU XIAN:

STOP CALLING ME THAT!

ACOLYTE:

Let's go to the meditation garden.

[*The* ACOLYTE *gathers up the vegetarian dish and* XU XIAN *and departs. Music.* NARRATOR TWO *enters. In the distance we see* WHITE *and* GREEN SNAKE *approaching.* WHITE SNAKE *is "poling" their invisible boat with a length of bamboo. They are dressed in their fighting gear and wear their "swords"—short lengths of bamboo—tucked in the back of their sashes.*]

NARRATOR TWO:

So many things go wrong in this life. Trying to be polite, being impressed with authority, and even having too strong a love of poetry have landed Xu Xian in this predicament. The monks like to say there are no problems, only situations: yet, here comes Lady Bai with her companion Greenie, on a boat made from her hairpin, coming to confront Fa Hai. That is indeed a situation.

[NARRATOR TWO *takes the bamboo pole from the ladies to turn it into the monastery gate. The ladies pass under the gate into the monastery.* SECOND ACOLYTE *enters, passing by. The sound of the bell continues.*]

WHITE SNAKE:
Now Greenie, remember, it's best to contain your—

GREEN SNAKE [*to* SECOND ACOLYTE]:
You there! Has a Master Xu come here?

SECOND ACOLYTE:
Pardon me?

GREEN SNAKE:
When they shaved your head did they shave your ears off, too?

WHITE SNAKE:
Greenie—

GREEN SNAKE [*writing the characters in the air*]:
MAS–TER XU?

SECOND ACOLYTE:
Oh . . . we're not supposed to say. Oops. Oh, dear.

GREEN SNAKE:
Not supposed to say what?

WHITE SNAKE:
Not supposed to say what?

SECOND ACOLYTE:
Oh, dear.

WHITE SNAKE:
Take us to him!

SECOND ACOLYTE:
You'd better see the Abbott.

[*As he speaks,* NARRATOR TWO *uses the pole to create the laby-rinthine hallways of the monastery. He extends it horizontally. The* SECOND ACOLYTE *accompanies the ladies along the path of the pole then grabs the far end of the pole and switches its angle by ninety degrees to make a bend in the hallway. The ladies pass her, continu-ing down the hallway until they arrive in* FA HAI's *chamber.*]

NARRATOR TWO:
The terrified acolyte led them through the labyrinth of the Golden Monastery until they reached a private room where Fa Hai sat in deep meditation . . . apparently.

[NARRATOR TWO *and* SECOND ACOLYTE *exit with the pole.*]

CONFRONTATION AT THE TEMPLE

[FA HAI *is sitting with his back to* WHITE SNAKE *and* GREEN SNAKE.]

WHITE SNAKE:
Bai Suzhen pays her respects to the Reverend Abbott Fa H—

FA HAI:

I know who—or what—you are. The only question is why you've come clouding the pure air of the Golden Monastery?

WHITE SNAKE:

Reverend sir, we have come to escort my husband, Xu Xian, home from your honored temple.

FA HAI:

Xu Xian will never leave this place.

WHITE SNAKE:

Whatever can you mean? Is he ill? Or injured somehow? Bring me to—

FA HAI [*standing*]:

Quite the opposite, madam. He has been cured. Xu Xian has seen through the illusion of the world and prostrated himself at the feet of my unworthy self. He has taken holy orders.

WHITE SNAKE:
What?

GREEN SNAKE [*scoffing*]:
Master Xu? A monk?!

WHITE SNAKE:
That can't be.

FA HAI:
It is true. He has renounced the world.

WHITE SNAKE:

Renounced the wor—? But he has a home and a pharmaceuticals business to take care of! Please, reverend, call him here quickly so that he and I may disc—

FA HAI:

Out of the question. You will never see Xu Xian in this life, in this world, again. So slide on back to Mount Emei and forget you ever meddled in the affairs of men. You have come to the end of your evil influence.

[FA HAI *begins to leave.*]

GREEN SNAKE:

Stop talking nonsense! You're the evil influence—breaking up a happy home!

FA HAI:

Home? That immoral alliance?

GREEN SNAKE:

Because you're so lonely and miserable yourself!

FA HAI:

Ha!

WHITE SNAKE:

Greenie!

GREEN SNAKE:

It's true, mistress! No one who is truly happy in his own life cares a bean about the "morals" of others!

WHITE SNAKE:

Mind your manners! Reverend—I don't understand: my husband and I are expecting a child. He would never voluntarily become a monk—

FA HAI:

You think if he ever glimpsed just one scale of your true slimy self he wouldn't come tearing up this mountain as fast as his feet could carry him? And as to that thing you're carrying—you think your husband wants a monster burning incense for him when he's dead?

GREEN SNAKE:

Now you're slandering a little baby? The only monster here is you, you fat pile of orange—

WHITE SNAKE [*pulling* GREEN SNAKE *away from* FA HAI]:
Greenie! [*To* FA HAI] Sir Abbot, even if Xu Xian is to stay here, well, I accept that. But there are just a few things—business things—to tie up with him. Won't you call him—

FA HAI:

Who do you think I am? A gullible mouse like that husband of yours? A leaf, for you to blow on and push about where you will?

WHITE SNAKE:

But if you would just—

FA HAI:

Get out! Before I kill you!

WHITE SNAKE:

You may kill me, but I will see my husband!

[GREEN SNAKE *jumps between* FA HAI *and* WHITE SNAKE, *drawing her sword.*]

GREEN SNAKE:
I'll kill you first!

FA HAI:
You insolent viper! I'll beat you to death!

WHITE SNAKE [*intervening and kneeling*]:
Sir Abbott! I must remind you—you are a high-ranking clergyman! A man of nonviolence! Of compassion—

FA HAI:
Be quiet. This is a place sacred to Buddha. If you do not get out of here at once, there will not be enough pieces of you left to bury.

[WHITE SNAKE, *under the pressure of her intense emotions, begins to revert to her snake nature. She begins to slither and hiss. A slow, distorted music begins and builds.*]

WHITE SNAKE:
Reverend Fa Hai, you are dessseptive, violent, and utterly without compassion. I have asssked you reasonably and quietly to let me ssssee my husband but I ssssee you are intent on dessstroying all of usss. It is clear that only one of usss can live upon this earth! [*Rising and drawing her sword*] I call on the spirits of the sea! Rise up and flood this temple!

[*The* WATER SPIRITS *enter with very long blue sleeves.*]

FA HAI:
And I call on the spirits of the air to defeat you—you devil monsters!

[*The* CLOUD SPIRITS *enter carrying clouds.*]

THE WATER BATTLE

[*Music. Drumming. The* WATER SPIRITS *spin and twirl their enormously long blue silk sleeves. The* CLOUD SPIRITS *dash by with their clouds. In slow motion* WHITE SNAKE *and* GREEN SNAKE *engage* FA HAI *in battle. The* WATER SPIRITS *and* CLOUD SPIRITS *pursue each other around the central fighters.* WHITE SNAKE *falls away to the ground.* GREEN SNAKE *is left alone to battle* FA HAI. *Finally, the blue sleeves of the* WATER SPIRITS *are detached to become waves. These silk waves rise and fall around* FA HAI *until he is overcome by them. He is pulled offstage by and with all the* SPIRITS. *The music drops out but drumming continues, insistent and driving.* WHITE SNAKE *is moaning on the ground.* GREEN SNAKE *dashes up to her.*]

THE STORM

GREEN SNAKE:
Mistress, are you wounded?

WHITE SNAKE:
No, it's the baby. I think the baby is coming!

GREEN SNAKE:
Oh no! Not now!

WHITE SNAKE:

But tell me! How is the battle going? Are our Water Spirits victorious?

GREEN SNAKE:

Madam, I believe they are—I saw Fa Hai himself swept away. Surely he is drowned!

WHITE SNAKE:

Then give the order to retreat—Ooooo!

GREEN SNAKE:

Mistress, quick! The tempests are out of control. We must find our little boat and climb aboard!

[*Drumming continues.* WHITE SNAKE *and* GREEN SNAKE *move upstage.* WHITE SNAKE *sits and rocks back and forth in their invisible boat as* GREEN SNAKE *stands, holding a tattered white parasol as a sail or rudder. Downstage, the* ACOLYTE *and* XU XIAN *enter; they are in a corridor of the monastery. They shout through the drumming and cymbal crashes, the sound of which periodically knocks them to the ground.*]

XU XIAN:

Brother, what is going on?

ACOLYTE:

Oh, Brother Xu, remember that all is illusion—

XU XIAN:

Yes, yes, I know—but what is that tremendous din?

ACOLYTE:

Your wife came up to the temple—

XU XIAN:
In this ferocious storm?

ACOLYTE:
No, no Brother Xu, your wife *brought* the storm!

XU XIAN:
What?

ACOLYTE:
She is battling against Fa Hai.

XU XIAN:
My wife?!

ACOLYTE:
Yes, she conjured all the Water Spirits—the crabs and fishes of the sea, the seahorses and the clams.

XU XIAN:
My wife?!

ACOLYTE:
For you, Brother Xu—she is flooding the mountain! Oh, Brother Xu, I am so moved by this display of tender affection. I know that we must give up our attachments to the world, but still [*coming to a momentous conclusion*] it was wrong of Fa Hai to force you to become a monk!

XU XIAN:
Will you help me?

ACOLYTE:
Follow me, Brother Xu!

[*They exit. The wind blows the parasol from* GREEN SNAKE's *hands. She sits down behind* WHITE SNAKE, *embracing her as they ride the wild river.*]

GREEN SNAKE:
Mistress, be careful, we've lost our rudder.

WHITE SNAKE [*groans*]:
Where are we? I don't recognize a thing! Everything is underwater.

GREEN SNAKE:
Oh, mistress, stay calm! But I think the pharmacy is far behind us. Shall we try to turn around? The current is very strong—

WHITE SNAKE:
No, you're right—the current is far too strong. And those spirits of the air might pursue us straight to our home. Let's let the boat keep drifting all the way—let it take us where it will.

[WHITE SNAKE *groans loudly.*]

GREEN SNAKE:
Hold on, mistress! Here we go!

[*The word "go" extends into a prolonged cry that is joined by* WHITE SNAKE. *Drumming gives way to swirling music.* NARRATOR TWO *enters, dragging a pole behind him. This will become the Broken Bridge.*]

NARRATOR TWO:

The swollen river and the winds swirled them about like leaves caught in a courtyard. Hour after hour they plunged through the foaming waters, never knowing where they were until, at last . . .

[*The music softens and calms.*]

GREEN SNAKE:

Look, mistress! The Broken Bridge. Do you see?

WHITE SNAKE:

Yes.

GREEN SNAKE:

Do you remember what you said when we first saw it?

WHITE SNAKE:

"It isn't broken at all!"

GREEN SNAKE:

That's right. We're back at the West Lake, where we first came down our mountain.

WHITE SNAKE:

And there's the willow were we first saw Xu Xian. Greenie, try to head there. We were saved there once before in a storm.

[WHITE *and* GREEN SNAKE *reach for the pole and drag themselves along it as* NARRATOR TWO *pulls it forward.*]

So they navigated as best they could, toward that lonely spot, deserted and damp, until at last they reached the shore.

[WHITE *and* GREEN SNAKE *collapse on the shore. Music shifts again.*]

And what of Xu Xian? Here the story forks again like the forks of the Yangtze River.

[XU XIAN *and* ACOLYTE *enter.*]

Some say it was the little Acolyte who freed Xu Xian and he made his way on his own; first back to the pharmacy and then on to the West Lake.

[XU XIAN *and the* ACOLYTE *freeze, and* GUAN YIN *enters with several performers carrying the large cloud silk.*]

But others say it was Guan Yin, the compassionate, who rolled him down that mountain on a cloud, right to the foot of the Broken Bridge.

[*Pause.*]

Let's go for the cloud.

[*Music swells.* GUAN YIN *comes forward followed by the performers who carry the cloud over* XU XIAN's *head, then roll it back toward his feet. He steps onto the cloth and rolls over it as it circles back over his head. This happens twice. Finally, the cloud deposits him on the shore near* WHITE *and* GREEN SNAKE. *The performers pull the cloud*

off in a great flurry and depart. The underscoring that has contin-
ued since the beginning of the water battle finally ends.]

AT BROKEN BRIDGE

XU XIAN:
My dear! Greenie! Is it really you?

WHITE SNAKE:
Good heavens, Xu Xian!

XU XIAN:
Thanks be to Heaven and Earth, I have found you at last! My dear,
are you wounded?

GREEN SNAKE [*approaching* XU XIAN, *threatening*]:
You have a nerve, coming here to ask that! You treacherous, faith-
less villain! It's your fault my mistress is in this state! You don't deserve to live!

[GREEN SNAKE *raises her sword to him. Music. Everything stops.*
NARRATOR FIVE *enters with his spectacles and book.* GREEN SNAKE
slowly performs the gesture NARRATOR FIVE *describes, then slowly*
raises her sword even higher to strike XU XIAN.]

NARRATOR FIVE:
Secrets of the Chinese Drama. Hand Gesture Number Four: The
Fighting Fist.

Bend the four fingers and press the thumb tightly against the middle joint of the middle finger, with the index finger curved above the

120

thumb. The tip of the little finger should not touch the third finger because a tight fist does not look artistic. This gesture is seldom performed by a female character, with the exception of "The Meeting at Broken Bridge," where the maid raises her fist against her master for his desertion of the White Snake lady.

[*Music ends.* NARRATOR FIVE *departs as* GREEN SNAKE *accelerates out of slow motion to strike.*]

GREEN SNAKE:
AaaaaaaAAAAAAHHHH!

[XU XIAN *leaps up and* GREEN SNAKE *chases him around in a big circle.*]

XU XIAN:
Greenie! Greenie, what has come over you!

WHITE SNAKE:
Greenie, stop this!

XU XIAN:
Have mercy!

WHITE SNAKE:
We must listen to his explanation!

[XU XIAN *collapses on the floor.* GREEN SNAKE *looms over him.*]

GREEN SNAKE:
All right. I'll ask the questions. How did my mistress treat you?

XU XIAN:
With surpassing kindness!

GREEN SNAKE:

Then why did you betray her, sneaking off to Golden Mountain to become a monk—siding with Fa Hai against her!

WHITE SNAKE [*struggling to her feet, holding her belly, very angry*]:
Yes, why! Why? From the day we met I've brought you nothing but good fortune. You were an assistant, and I made you the owner of a shop. You were a boarder in your sister's house, and I gave you your own roof—never asking anything in return but your affection. But in spite of your vow you went off with Fa Hai. Even if you care nothing for me, you should have had some thought for the child I'm carrying. You—you stony-hearted villain! You caused me almost to lose my life!

XU XIAN:
Both of you do me wrong!

GREEN SNAKE:
Oh, *we've* done *you* wrong?

XU XIAN:
Yes. Fa Hai is cunning! He pretended . . . he pretended that what he had told me before wasn't true at all and invited me up to the monastery to view the leaves to make amends.

GREEN SNAKE:
To view leaves?

XU XIAN:
Yes, and then he locked the gate. I was a prisoner.

WHITE SNAKE:
You were? A prisoner?

GREEN SNAKE:
Don't listen to him!

XU XIAN:
Yes! In a dark cell! With vegetarian dishes!

WHITE SNAKE:
Oh, my poor darling!

GREEN SNAKE [*to* WHITE SNAKE]:
Mistress! [*To* XU XIAN] How did you escape then?

XU XIAN [*confused, struggling*]:
I can't rightly say: an acolyte helped me, but then I believe it was the intervention of Guan Yin . . .

GREEN SNAKE:
Mistress, do not be taken in by this!

XU XIAN:
I swear it is the truth. May Heaven strike me down if it is not!

GREEN SNAKE:
Oh, another of his great vows!

WHITE SNAKE:
No, Greenie. I believe him and you should too. Do you?

GREEN SNAKE [*hesitating*]:
Oh . . . I suppose. He's just that gullible.

[GREEN SNAKE *sits down at a little distance.*]

XU XIAN:
Thank you, thank you.

WHITE SNAKE:
Only, now you must go.

XU XIAN:
What?

[WHITE SNAKE *goes to sit apart from* XU XIAN, *her back to him. Music rises slowly under her confession.*]

WHITE SNAKE:
There is something that lies between us. You know it is true. Something . . . hidden. You will always suspect it and I will always live in fear of that suspicion. Always be on my guard; and I will end up risking my life again, and the life of this child, all in order to keep things as they are.

GREEN SNAKE:
It's true, mistress. You're right to finally say it. And now that you have—Master Xu, we bid you farewell. You must leave us now.

[GREEN SNAKE *goes to sit with* WHITE SNAKE. *They sit formally, on their knees, their backs to* XU XIAN, *facing the audience. Music ends.*]

XU XIAN:
My love?

WHITE SNAKE:
Greenie is right, you must go.

GREEN SNAKE:

Go, Master Xu, and we will return to where we came from as well.

XU XIAN:

If that is your wish, then I will go. But listen to me first—I must have my say. Almost from the day we met, I was plagued by doubt. When I first came to the red house in the west I almost did not come in. And when Greenie proposed marriage between us I again felt it was not right, but I ignored those feelings. Then Fa Hai came and those doubts were reawakened. After the Dragon Boat Festival I don't believe I was completely fooled by you and Greenie, but again, I ignored those doubts and allowed myself to be blinded to your true nature. But now, I have seen with my own eyes what you did for me at the Golden Monastery and I have no doubt at all.

GREEN SNAKE:

You see, mistress—

[Music begins again.]

XU XIAN:

I have no doubt that no man has ever been loved as I have been loved. I have no doubt that I know you as you truly are; I have no doubt that you are, in fact, partly a snake, partly a spirit; and I ask you to forgive me for ever doubting you at all.

WHITE SNAKE:

Am I dreaming?

XU XIAN:

Whatever world is yours, I want that world. Please, say that you forgive me for my weakness and my blindness that made you feel you had to hide; and take me home, wherever that may be.

[*Slowly,* WHITE SNAKE *moves to* XU XIAN *and they embrace. Then it is clear the baby is coming. The music rises and shifts to the introduction of the Lantern Festival Song. The three exit as* NARRATOR THREE *enters carrying a lantern. Many members of the company follow, all carrying lanterns.*]

THE LANTERN FESTIVAL

[*Song.*]

NARRATOR THREE:
Both urgent and gentle,
Late autumn leaves are falling.
The baby is coming.
The old year slips away.

COMPANY:
Go on home, Bai Suzhen,
Go on home.
Go on home, Bai Suzhen,
Go on home.
Go on home.

ALL:
Light up the lanterns
For the brand new year is here.
New clothes and a new life;
Three friends are now four.

Light the lanterns, Xu Xian,
Light the lamps.

Light the lanterns, Xu Xian,
Light the lamps.
Light the lamps.

[XU XIAN, WHITE SNAKE, *and* GREEN SNAKE *enter. They are in their festival finery, their New Year's clothes.* GREEN SNAKE *carries the baby.*]

The stars shine up above,
The lanterns sway below.
The river and her eyes give back
The enchanted glow.

Go and stroll, young lovers,
Go and stroll.
Go and stroll, young lovers,
Go and stroll.
Go and stroll.

[*The company continues to stroll around with the lanterns. Gradually, one by one, several leave the stage.*]

WHITE SNAKE:
Look at everyone in their festival finery! And all the lanterns!—just like glow worms in the night.

GREEN SNAKE:
Less tasty, though.

WHITE SNAKE:
Greenie! [*Laughs.*] But really, has there ever been anything so pretty?

XU XIAN:

They pale next to you, my dear. You are the moon that makes the stars fade away. But . . . are you truly well enough for this walking about? Be honest.

WHITE SNAKE:

It's exactly one month since Dream Dragon was born—and the New Year's lantern festival falling on the same day? What could be more auspicious for my very first going out? I wouldn't miss this double-happiness for the world if— [*looking around, and then privately to Xu Xian*] I had to crawl to it on my belly.

XU XIAN [*laughs privately with her*]:
All right!

[*He catches sight of his reflection and* WHITE SNAKE'*s in the water.*]

We look like lovers on our wedding day, don't we? Or how a bride and groom should look—we never did.

GREEN SNAKE:

Well, if you want to get married again, you've got a little gentleman to hold the bride's train.

XU XIAN:

We won't need the young man's services. But I'm sure you will when you get married!

GREEN SNAKE:

Master Xu! I've told you! *Never* say things like that to me!!

XU XIAN [*teasing, merciless*]:
I'll be your go-between . . .

WHITE SNAKE AND GREEN SNAKE:
Stop it!

XU XIAN:
I know an auspicious date!

GREEN SNAKE:
Master Xu! I'm serious!

XU XIAN:
Are you going to chase me in a circle again?

GREEN SNAKE [*making a "fighting fist"*]:
I just might!

[XU XIAN *laughs as* GREEN SNAKE *playfully chases him around.*]

WHITE SNAKE:
Stop running with the baby! You two! Stop teasing her and apologize!

[*They stop.* XU XIAN *bows.*]

XU XIAN:
You have an abject apology from this miserable Xu Xian.

[*They all come together and look at the baby.*]

WHITE SNAKE:
This is a moment I wish would last forever.

[FA HAI *enters disguised as a beggar. He speaks in a feeble voice.*]

FA HAI:
Alms for the poor. In the name of Buddha!

XU XIAN:
Do you have any coins with you, my dear?

[*The remaining company members gather around* FA HAI, *each giving him a coin and exiting. This activity helps to hide him from* WHITE *and* GREEN SNAKE *and* XU XIAN.]

FA HAI:
Alms in the name of Buddha.

WHITE SNAKE:
Oh, let me see . . . One moment, sir . . .

GREEN SNAKE [*suddenly seeing*]:
Mistress—no . . . *no!*

[FA HAI *reveals himself and flourishes the magical Lingshan Bowl. Two of the* CLOUD SPIRITS *rush forward from behind him with a long length of golden fabric that ensnares* WHITE SNAKE *and pulls her to the ground as the* CLOUD SPIRITS *rush back upstage.* GREEN SNAKE *thrusts the baby into* XU XIAN's *arms and prepares to fight* FA HAI. *Throughout the following,* WHITE SNAKE *is dragged away, slowly, slowly.* FA HAI *holds the bowl extended, casting a sort of force field that holds* GREEN SNAKE *and* XU XIAN *at bay.*]

WHITE SNAKE:
What isss happening? What hasss happened!

[*Writhing in the golden ray,* WHITE SNAKE *begins to revert to her snake form.*]

FA HAI:
You think you could defeat me, you miserable witch!

GREEN SNAKE:
    Mistress!

WHITE SNAKE:
        What issssssss it?

FA HAI:
You think you could drown Fa Hai with your scaly cousins of the sea? Your little clams and crabs and fishes? You gave me a lovely bath—that's all!

XU XIAN:
Stop it!

WHITE SNAKE:
What'ssssssss happening?

FA HAI:
This is the magic Lingshan Bowl, my dear, capable of trapping any monster in its sacred ray. It took me a month of ceaseless searching, but I found it, and now you've found your doom!

GREEN SNAKE:
You're the monster! You're the only monster here!

XU XIAN:
Let her go!

GREEN SNAKE:
You fat devil!

WHITE SNAKE:
Greenie!

FA HAI:
Your mistress is finished and you are nothing—

WHITE SNAKE:
Greenie, go! Fly away!

GREEN SNAKE:
Never, madam!—

FA HAI:
Crawl on off!

GREEN SNAKE:
I'll die first and take this one with me!

[GREEN SNAKE *is on the ground, reaching toward* WHITE SNAKE. WHITE SNAKE *speaks with tremendous effort, with her last ounce of strength. She is still being pulled away.*]

WHITE SNAKE:
I command you, Greenie, with all my power, I command you to leave me now!

GREEN SNAKE:
But—

WHITE SNAKE [*quietly*]:
It'ssss over, Greenie. Back to the mountainsssss and the treesssssss . . .

[GREEN SNAKE *runs off.*]

XU XIAN [*kneeling*]:
Sir Abbot, listen to me. My only desire is to be with her.

FA HAI:
It is unnatural! It is not the way!

XU XIAN:
Stop saying that! That's just something you're saying!—

FA HAI:
I say it because it is so!

XU XIAN:
It is not so—!

WHITE SNAKE:
Xu Xian, don't argue . . . hopelesssssss—

XU XIAN:
But Lord Abbott, if you will have mercy on this child and on his mother, I will do whatever you ask. I will take the vows of a monk.

WHITE SNAKE:
Don't beg him, Xu Xian. Don't give another breath to him. There'sss not a drop of mersssy in him.

FA HAI:

How dare you! This is all an act of mercy! I'm saving him from damnation. Mortals don't marry spirits, men don't marry snakes!

WHITE SNAKE:

You're a butcher in a monk's robes!

FA HAI:

Not another word! [*Raising his arms*] Spirits of the air take this beast and place her beneath the Thunder Peak Pagoda! There she will suffer forever!

[*A* CLOUD SPIRIT *enters with a many-storied parasol that he plants in the stage.*]

XU XIAN:

No! No!

WHITE SNAKE:

Xu Xian! Take care of the baby, do you hear me?

FA HAI:

Oh, how touching.

WHITE SNAKE:

Take care of the baby!

FA HAI:

Amithabha Buddha!

[WHITE SNAKE *is dragged off the stage.* FA HAI *exits.*]

CONCLUSION

[*Everything is quiet.* XU XIAN *is alone on the stage with* NARRATOR TWO.]

NARRATOR TWO:

By all accounts, Fa Hai did what he said. He put poor Lady Bai beneath the Thunder Peak Pagoda and kept her there, for a very long while indeed. But here, for the last time, our story forks, like the branches of the willow at Broken Bridge.

[*Music.* XU XIAN *exits.* NARRATOR ONE *and* NARRATOR FIVE *enter.* NARRATOR FIVE *carries a bucket with a little rice. Throughout the following narration, in silhouette against a pure white backdrop, the figures enter and perform the actions as they are described.*]

NARRATOR ONE:

Some say that after many years, Dream Dragon, the son of Bai Suzhen and Xu Xian, grew to be a great scholar. He came one day, knelt, and prayed at Thunder Peak Pagoda and this demonstration of filial piety crumbled the pagoda and so his mother was freed.

[DREAM DRAGON *lifts the pagoda parasol as someone else embodies* WHITE SNAKE *in her parasol-head-only form. This* WHITE SNAKE *and her son exit. The pagoda parasol is replaced.*]

NARRATOR TWO:

Others say nothing at all about the son, but say it was someone else [GREEN SNAKE *enters*], someone who quietly spent the next seven centuries studying upon a mountain until at last her magic skill had grown unimaginably vast [GREEN SNAKE *strikes a graceful pose*], almost as big as her heart. Elegant, graceful, patient, and kind, it was Greenie who came to free her.

[GREEN SNAKE *reaches under the pagoda parasol and tenderly seems to pick up the very small, wooden snake used in* GUAN YIN's *narration of* WHITE SNAKE's *past life (it was hidden in her sleeve). She exits.*]

NARRATOR FIVE:
But what of Xu Xian?

[XU XIAN *enters. He is old, bent over, using a cane. He walks very slowly toward the parasol pagoda.*]

Not much is said. He sold the pharmacy and "donated" the money to the magistrate whence it had come. He went back to being an assistant, and living with his sister and his brother-in-law. He did not remarry. For the rest of his life, on his days off, he walked by the Thunder Peak Pagoda and thought of her, and of that brief happy time.

[XU XIAN *has reached the pagoda parasol.*]

NARRATOR TWO:
But you must not feel sorry for Xu Xian.

NARRATOR ONE:
With enough time and distance all forking paths come to the same place.

[*All members of the company except* WHITE SNAKE *come onstage quietly and kneel.* NARRATORS ONE, TWO, *and* FIVE *kneel as well.* XU XIAN *puts down his cane.*]

NARRATOR TWO:

In fact they never forked at all. In the hour of our death, when the heart uncoils, we can, at last, see that all ideas of separation, loss, difference are nothing but illusion.

[WHITE SNAKE *appears in the distance, far downstage or in the aisle of the theater, in her most splendid human form, holding the red parasol, folded.* XU XIAN *sees her. Throughout the following she and* XU XIAN *move slowly toward each other.*]

NARRATOR ONE:

We are greeted and ushered home, back into the whole, by whatever image we most loved in our time on earth, which held for us, whether we knew it or not, the symbol of divine reunion.

NARRATOR ONE:

There is no limit to what form this may take:

BOATMAN:

a boy

ACOLYTE:

or a girl,

GREEN SNAKE:

a snake,

NARRATOR FIVE:

a dog,

NARRATOR THREE:

the form of light itself,

GUAN YIN:

the wind in the trees,

NARRATOR THREE:

the way the grass looks when the sun is going down and all the riot
of insects play,

FA HAI:

the water as it ripples on the surface of a lake.

NARRATOR ONE:

Or, in this case, a young woman with her arm outstretched, returning an umbrella.

[WHITE SNAKE *opens the umbrella as she reaches* XU XIAN. *They embrace. She holds the umbrella above them. Music ends. Pause.*]

NARRATOR TWO:

Don't be afraid. It is impossible to die alone.

[NARRATOR FIVE *lets fall a small stream of rice into his bucket as the
stage darkens. It is the rain.*]

A NOTE ON CASTING

The White Snake could probably be performed with slightly fewer or a great many more actors than the original eleven. Because the play was written in the same time frame as it was rehearsed, there was not as much careful thought behind which narrator is assigned what text as one might assume. The division of the minor narration apart from Narrators One and Two may be assigned differently, and your singers need not necessarily be the narrators as they are listed in the text. However, I would caution against using a barrage of too many different narrative voices; it is a difficult thing for the audience to have to constantly make that switch. The individual actor's tracks as they are described below could also be distributed differently. In addition to the eleven actors, there were three live musicians: a cellist, a flute and other woodwind player, and a percussion and string player.

FIRST WOMAN: White Snake

SECOND WOMAN: Green Snake

THIRD WOMAN: Guan Yin, Second Acolyte, Water Spirit

FOURTH WOMAN: Narrator One, Visitor One, Sister, Master Lin, Madame Lin, Xu Xian, Cloud Spirit

FIFTH WOMAN: Narrator Three, Visitor Five, Doubt, Crane Spirit, Water Spirit

SIXTH WOMAN: Acolyte, Visitor Two

FIRST MAN: Xu Xian, Merchant

SECOND MAN: Fa Hai, Narrator Four, Visitor Four

THIRD MAN: Narrator Two, Visitor Two, Brother-in-Law, Stag Spirit, Cloud Spirit

FOURTH MAN: Boatman, The Moon, Night Watchman, Master Wu, Dream Dragon, Cloud Spirit

FIFTH MAN: Narrator Five, Master Liang, Canopus, Cloud Spirit

APPENDIX: ADDITIONAL NOTES ON THE STAGING OF *THE WHITE SNAKE*

These elaborations on the design for *The White Snake* are intended only as clarification of what was done in the original production at the Oregon Shakespeare Festival, not as a prescription for what must happen in any subsequent production. The play can be performed with next to nothing, or with puppets, music, and projections of your own devising.

THE SNAKE PUPPETS

The snake puppets were made with dryer venting hose covered in fabric, a bit of sculpted foam for the tail, a Styrofoam head, and two dowels attached about eighteen inches from either end of the snake. White Snake had a little magnet hidden in her "mouth" so that the rat and the ganoderma herb (both with magnets inside) could attach to her. If you use this method, you will need to experiment with the length of the snakes to see what works best: the dryer venting hose contracts and expands.

PROJECTIONS

Following is a chronological description of the projections used in the original production of *The White Snake*. The show might easily be done without projections, with or without some additional design elements to replace them. If you do use them, you might use entirely different images or techniques, but I strongly recommend against using projections to substitute for a more handcrafted, old-fashioned stage embodiment of the magic of White Snake, the sea battle, or any other part of the stage action. Projections should be used sparingly and should be subtle, poetic, slightly abstracted, and never the focal point of the stage picture. The images are not necessarily static throughout the scenes. Where no image is described below, the screen was dark, or lit and toned with color in the conventional way through stage lighting.

The opening image was front projected onto the white silk show curtain that masks the stage before the play, but all the rest of the images were rear projected on an upstage screen, requiring a performance space of some depth.

OPENING

First, a black brush painting of bamboo leaves and the Chinese characters for "White Snake" is projected onto the white silk show drop masking the stage. After the curtain drops, slow moving gray clouds appear on the rear screen. They remain, in various states of light or darkness, until White Snake and Greenie journey to the West Lake.

AT WEST LAKE

The audience sees scant brush lines of the mountains of West Lake and the Thunder Peak Pagoda in the distance. Willow branches move slightly in the foreground.

TWO HOMES

When White Snake and Greenie arrive at the ruin of a house, the image is of a dark, bare branch against a dark green background. When White Snake transforms the ruin of the old, unseen "house," the branch blossoms with red flowers and the background becomes golden.

MARRIAGE

During the song "The Evening Light," the screen darkens from deep blue to black and the branch fades, leaving only the image of the blossoms, which turn from red to white, like stars. During the song "My Heart is Blooming," the white blossoms turn red again and begin to fall. The screen is filled with eternally falling red petals against a black background throughout the encounter between Xu Xian and White Snake.

OPENING OF THE PHARMACY AND THE COMING OF FA HAI

Whenever we are in the pharmacy, the image on screen is a Chinese ink drawing of a town viewed from an elevated angle. The first time this appears, the image appears to "pour out" from the lower center of the screen like spilled ink.

When Narrator Two introduces the Golden Monastery and as the citizens enter, the image dissolves to a Chinese painting, a view of mountains with the Golden Monastery in the mid-distance.

DRAGON BOAT FESTIVAL

A colorful distortion of wooden dragon boat prows is projected onto the side walls of the set. A bright blue day is on the back screen.

THE KUNLUN FOREST

The pattern and image of the bamboo poles hanging over the stage is repeated on the screen, amid a bright green color field.

FA HAI LURES XU XIAN

As Xu Xian leaves his house to settle something with a client, a single large yellow maple leaf appears in the corner of a field of blue.

As Xu Xian and Fa Hai board the boat, the screen darkens and the image of the maple leaf dissolves to swirling clouds; the clouds gradually resolve into the ink drawing of the Monastery and distant landscape.

THE WATER BATTLE

For the Water Battle the backdrop is of pure, bright blue. As White Snake and Greenie make their escape on the boat, stylized blue waves painted in the Chinese manner start to rise, and a little army of eighteenth-century drawings of crabs begins to move sideways across the screen.

AT BROKEN BRIDGE

The West Lake image reappears, but the willow branches are still and bare; the color is dull gray, washed out.

THE LANTERN FESTIVAL

Dozens of illuminated Chinese lamps, large and slow, float upward in a repeated pattern against a dark background. When Fa Hai deploys the Lingshan bowl, the lanterns disappear and the screen is black.

CONCLUSION

All the characters enacting various versions of the conclusion are silhouetted against a white screen.

MUSIC

Three musicians sat in front of the raised stage, visible to the audience but not interfering with the action of the play. One musician played cello, one played a variety of woodwinds, and one played pipa, drums, cymbals, and gongs. The music for the show was recorded and can be obtained by contacting Ronnie Malley at ronnie.malley@gmail.com. However, this recording does not contain every cue and was not made with the intention of serving for further productions. License for the original music can be applied for through Andre Pluess (drdre@red-bean.com).

THE CABINET

The entire design for *The White Snake* is simplicity itself, except for the very elaborate Chinese medicine cabinet. This was a sort of trick box that lived below the stage and could rise to various heights by means of a mechanical lift. Its top surface was painted to appear as part of the stage floor; its upstage side was curtained, but actually entirely open. At various heights it served as a full-sized medicine cabinet, a counter in the shop, or a bed. It had several functioning drawers that contained the medicines of the pharmacy. When it was raised to full height, two central doors could open to reveal a sort of Chinese bed or miniature bedchamber, complete with a little hanging lamp, pillows, and satin curtains.

The principal magic of the cabinet is deployed when White Snake involuntarily resumes her natural shape after the Dragon Boat Festival. The actress playing White Snake entered the cabinet, closed the doors, and exited through its open back. Then, behind the closed doors, a false front about a foot deep was raised in front of the bedroom setting within the cabinet. This false front contained a giant snake coiled about itself, with a head that could be manipulated by the White Snake actress from behind. After this monster was revealed, the doors were closed again by the narrator, the false façade containing the snake lowered, and the actress playing White Snake climbed back into the bedroom setting within the cabinet.

The cabinet worked well and was beautiful, but it requires a stage with a very deep trap space. The show may be performed more easily with a cabinet of fixed height (probably counter height) that rolls on, and with a separate bed or no bed at all for Xu Xian after he dies. The transformation of White Snake might be accomplished in some other way, or simply transpire offstage, unseen by the audience. There is an argument to be made for never seeing what Xu Xian sees in that terrible moment.

White Snake studies (Ako and Amy Kim Waschke)

Green Snake (Tanya McBride) and White Snake (Amy Kim Waschke) on their mountain under the moon. The Moon (visible in the background, holding a white parasol) was played by Vin Kridakorn.

Sharing the boat (Vin Kridakorn, Tanya McBride, Amy Kim Waschke, and Christopher Livingston)

Doubt (Emily Sophia Knapp) assails Xu Xian (Christopher Livingston).

Xu Xian (Christopher Livingston) anticipates the Dragon Boat Festival that White Snake (Amy Kim Waschke) secretly dreads.

White Snake (Amy Kim Waschke) confronts the Crane Spirit (Emily Sophia Knapp).

Madame Lin (Lisa Tejero) visits the pharmacy, surprising White Snake (Amy Kim Waschke) and Green Snake (Tanya McBride) with her news.

The drowning of Fa Hai (Jack Willis)

Mary Zimmerman's credits as an adapter and a director include *Metamorphoses, The Arabian Nights, The Odyssey, Journey to the West, Eleven Rooms of Proust, Silk, The Secret in the Wings, Mirror of the Invisible World, Argonautika,* and *The Notebooks of Leonardo da Vinci.* Her work has been produced at the Lookingglass Theatre and Goodman Theatre of Chicago; on Broadway at Circle in the Square; in New York at Second Stage, the Brooklyn Academy of Music, and the Manhattan Theatre Club; at the Mark Taper Forum in Los Angeles; and at the McCarter, Berkeley Repertory, and Seattle Repertory as well as many other theaters around the country and abroad. She has also directed at the Metropolitan Opera. Zimmerman is the recipient of a MacArthur Fellowship and won a Tony Award for her direction of *Metamorphoses.* She is a professor of performance studies at Northwestern University.